"Professor Heussi?
I Thought You Were a Book"

"Professor Heussi? I Thought You Were a Book"

A Memoir of Memorable Theological Educators

1950–2009

ERIC W. GRITSCH

WIPF & STOCK · Eugene, Oregon

"PROFESSOR HEUSSI? I THOUGHT YOU WERE A BOOK"
A Memoir of Memorable Theological Educators, 1950–2009

Copyright © 2009 Eric W. Gritsch. All rights reserved. Except for brief quotations in critical publications or reviews, no part of this book may be reproduced in any manner without prior written permission from the publisher. Write: Permissions, Wipf and Stock Publishers, 199 W. 8th Ave., Suite 3, Eugene, OR 97401.

Wipf and Stock Publishers
199 W. 8th Ave., Suite 3
Eugene, OR 97401

www.wipfandstock.com

ISBN 13: 978-1-60608-794-7

Manufactured in the U.S.A.

Unless otherwise stated, Scripture quotations are from the New Revised Standard © 1989.

To Bonnie,
Spouse and Spice of my Life

and

In Memoriam,
Wilhelm Dantine (1911–1981)
Viktor Frankl (1905–1997)
Karl Barth (1886–1968)
Roland Bainton (1894–1984)

"Not many of you should become teachers. For you know that we who teach will be judged with greater strictness. For all of us make many mistakes."

—James 3:1–2

"Those who wait for the Lord shall renew their strength, they shall mount up with wings like eagles, they shall run and not be weary, they shall walk and not faint."

—Isaiah 40:30; Confirmation Epigram, 1945

Contents

Prologue / ix

PART ONE: Graduate Studies

1 Vienna University (1950–1952, 1955–1956) / 3
   Wilhelm Dantine • Viktor Frankl • Gustav Entz • Josef Bohatec

2 Zurich University (1952) / 14
   Eduard Schweizer • Emil Brunner • Carl Jung

3 Basel University (1952–1953) / 24
   Oskar Cullmann • Karl Barth • Heinrich Vogel • Walter Eichrodt • Karl Jaspers

4 Yale Divinity School (1954–1955, 1957–1959) / 40
   Claude Welch • Roland Bainton • Sidney Ahlstrom • Richard Niebuhr • Robert Calhoun • Hajo Holborn • Erich Dinkler

PART TWO: Excursions

5 Union Seminary, New York / 57
   Reinhold Niebuhr • Paul Tillich

6 Harvard / 62
   George Williams • Henry Horn • Krister Stendahl

PART THREE: Teaching

7   Wellesley College (1959–1961) / 71

Fred Denbeaux

8   Gettysburg Lutheran Seminary (1961–1994) / 74

Abdel Ross Wentz • Robert Jenson • Elizabeth Kübler-Ross • Jürgen Moltmann • Wolfhart Pannenberg • Hans Küng • Heinrich Bornkamm • Hans von Campenhausen • Will Campbell • Günther Gassmann • John Loose

PART FOUR: Special Engagements

9   International Congress for Luther Research (1964–2002) / 97

Lennart Pinomaa • Gustaf Wingren • Regin Prenter • Leif Grane • Tuomo Mannermaa • Bernhard Lohse • Gerhard Ebeling • Heiko Oberman • Martin Brecht • Oswald Bayer • Jaroslav Pelikan • Lewis Spitz • Otto Hermann Pesch

10   Lutheran-Catholic Dialogue (1971–1992) / 117

George Lindbeck • Arthur Carl Piepkorn • Gerhard Forde • John Reumann • Joseph Burgess • Raymond Brown • Joseph Fitzmyer • Avery Dulles • Carl Peter • George Tavard • Johannes Cardinal Willebrands

Postscript / 133

Bibliography / 137

Prologue

WHEN I CRAMMED IN 1956 for my MDiv examination in church history, I used the textbook of my generation, the *Compendium of Church History* (*Kompendium der Kirchengeschichte*).[1] Legend has it that its author, Karl Heussi, was invited only once to offer a guest lecture after his retirement in the 1950s. It was assumed that he would be as boring a lecturer as he was an author. But the University of Tübingen invited him anyway. Its most renowned theologian, Helmut Thielicke, is said to have welcomed him with the words, "Professor Heussi? I thought you were a book!"

I do not know how his one and only formal appearance "in the flesh" was perceived. Only close, existential encounters reveal what kind of mentors teachers can be. Students usually see professors from a distance in large lecture halls, or encounter their work in publications, never really knowing the person behind the thick eyeglasses or the small print. This is especially the case in European theological education where students have personal encounters with professors only at the time of final examinations, written and oral, for a degree; these examinations are scheduled at specific times during an academic year. Students choose them when they think they are ready; if they flunk one or all examinations they usually have two more opportunities to take them, thus adding one or more years to their course of study. Since ex-

1. Heussi, *Kompendium der Kirchengeschichte*, 11th rev. ed., 1957. First edition 1907. Paperback 1991.

aminations are tied to specific courses in the United States, students may meet their teachers more often; but close personal encounters are still rare. Candidates for the highest degree (PhD or ThD) usually come to know their "doctor father" quite well, and examinations for that degree are scheduled together, reflecting the European model.[2]

This is a memoir about memorable theological educators, in a narrow and broader sense, ranging from members of theological faculties to historians, philosophers, and psychiatrists in universities on two continents, Europe and North America. I had the good fortune of close encounters with quite a few of my teachers throughout my graduate studies in the 1950s in both Europe and the United States. In retrospect, it seems that during the decade after World War II there was still an existential interconnection of people, generated by a need to struggle against many odds. Having experienced the regime of Adolf Hitler and Russian army occupation in my native Austria, I had learned to survive by looking for advantages through personal connections. Hindsight tells me that I may have been pushed from one stage to another, echoing the promise of my confirmation epigram.[3] I applied this lesson in my studies, leading to a PhD at Yale University and to a teaching career. Graduate

---

2. See Gritsch, "European and American Theological Education: Appraisal and Comparison" in *The Boy from the Burgenland*, 186–98. In Austria, the equivalent of an MDiv (Master of Divinity) was a Cand. theol. (*candidatura theologiae*, "candidacy of theology"). It was the academic part of the candidacy for ordination, with formal examinations in biblical studies, church history, theology, and ethics. The "practical" part required examinations in catechesis, liturgy, preaching, and pastoral care, followed by one year of work as a vicar in a parish.

3. See epigram in introductory pages, and in my "Memoir," *The Boy*, part 1.

Prologue

studies also created lifelong friendships with a few other students who made a name for themselves: in Vienna, Dieter Knall, Presiding Bishop of the Austrian Lutheran-Reformed Church; in Basel, Brevard Childs, Old Testament scholar, Shirley Guthrie, a popular Presbyterian systematic theologian, and Konrad Vogel, a courageous bishop in Communist Eastern Germany; at Yale, Leander Keck, and Louis Martyn, New Testament scholars, James Holloway, ethicist, and Egil Grislis, church historian. During my career as a church historian, I continued to have close encounters with memorable minds at home and abroad. All of them provided invaluable building blocks for the house of learning in my life. Some "made my day," to parody popular filmmaker and actor Clint Eastwood;[4] they created decisive moments that enriched, indeed changed, my mind. Others taught me lessons in negative learning, illustrating that even "God-talk," theology, deteriorates under the conditions of earthly, corporal, and penultimate existence, thus generating the proverbial experience from the sublime to the ridiculous. But in the main, they became signposts on my road of learning and teaching which often leads farther than their roads did—thus disclosing the wisdom of the old adage: "We are dwarfs who stand on the shoulders of giants. That is why we can see more and further than they did."[5]

---

4. "Make my day." A saying of Inspector Harry Callahan before he gunned down a young robber who threatened to kill a kidnapped waitress in the 1983 movie *Sudden Impact* (first use of the phrase in the 1982 film *Vice Squad*).

5. Bernard of Charters (d. c. 1130), a French Platonic philosopher. The quotation is recorded in the treatise *The Metalogicon*, iii, 4 (1150) written by John Salisbury, an English philosopher, historian, and churchman.

Prologue

Basic higher academic degrees, Bachelor, Master, and Doctor, originated in medieval universities after examinations conducted in the form of debates. Professors developed theses which candidates for a degree had to defend in public. So university education began with close encounters between teachers and students. Bookishness came into being in 1450 with the improved printing press of John Gutenberg in Mainz, Germany—the beginning of long-distance learning. My theological education has been enriched not only by reading books, but also by meeting their authors, or encountering teachers, who published little, or nothing, yet became a living word, as it were. Such existential encounters made me aware of the many, various ways of teaching and learning. They are part and parcel of the vicissitudes of history, well described by my most favorite subject in church history, Martin Luther.

> All of our experience with history should teach us, when we look back, how badly human wisdom is betrayed when it relies on itself. For hardly anything happens the way it is planned. But everything turns out differently, and the opposite happens from what one thought should happen.[6]

The Table of Contents lists in chronological order the locations where I encountered memorable mentors: 1) as a student in graduate schools, 2) in excursions from Yale to Union Seminary in New York and to Harvard, 3) in my teaching career as a colleague of other theological educators, and 4) during special assignments. Their names appear again in bold capital letters when the encounters are nar-

---

6. Sermon on 1 Peter 5:5–11, 1544. Translation mine. *Dr. Martin Luthers Werke*, 22, 33.23–7.

Prologue

rated. But in the narrative and in footnotes I list titles that pinpoint what I learned. Biblical quotations are from The New Revised Standard Version. Unpublished translations are mine.

This memoir is dedicated to my spouse Bonnie, partner in theological dialogue, and to the four most influential theological educators in my life: Wilhelm Dantine, the Viennese "house father," who opened for me the door to theology; Viktor Frankl, the Viennese psychiatrist, who showed me how theology can make my life meaningful; Karl Barth, the Swiss theologian, who provided the best way to do theology; and Roland Bainton, the "doctor father," who guided me to the guild of church historians.

EWG
At the threshold of the sixtieth year
of my theological education,
Memorial Day, May 25, 2009

PART ONE

Graduate Studies

*"Getting a PhD is Like Getting a Children's Disease.
The Older You Get, the More Dangerous it is."*

1

Vienna University

(1950–1952, 1955–1956)

WHENEVER I ENCOUNTERED OLDER students who, after some time as pastors in a parish or as teachers in a parochial school, wanted me to recommend them for graduate studies leading to a PhD, I alerted them to a caveat I coined, based on my own experience, and on the experiences of friends and acquaintances who postponed their doctoral studies: "Getting a PhD is like getting a children's disease; the older you get the more dangerous it is."

After eight years of education (age ten to eighteen) in a classical secondary school (*Gymnasium*), I graduated in 1950 and matriculated at the Protestant Theological Faculty of the University of Vienna in the same year. Hindsight suggests that I may have been motivated by the calling of my father who had been a Lutheran pastor until he was drafted into the German army in 1941, went missing in action on the Russian front in 1945, and was declared dead in 1948 (based on delayed evidence about his death). It seemed to have been a good idea to follow his example. But it was one of many choices, and I was not really committed to become a pastor in a tiny minority church (94 percent of Austrians were Roman Catholics). But the church offered a generous scholarship with room and board (breakfast only) at its "Home for Theologians" (*Theologenheim*) near the university, trying to draft students into the ordained ministry like army recruiters do now for mercenary service.

I joined a group of about twenty candidates, sharing a room with another student, a refugee from Transylvania (a German Saxon region in Romania known as *Siebenbürgen*). He was a serious, organized mind who rose in the ministry to become a regional bishop and finally the Presiding Bishop of the small Lutheran-Reformed (Calvinist) Church. Much less serious than he, I began my new life like a butterfly, moving here and there to taste the juices of academic life. I attended lectures in theology, philosophy, and history, feeling footloose and adventurous even though Austria was still occupied by troops in the military alliance of England, France, Russia, and the United States.[1] Moreover, Vienna offered quality music, fine arts, and many other ways of entertainment (I liked opera, using the cheap "standing-room"); and there were soirees in taverns or cafés with other students, not all of them studying theology for the ordained ministry.

The Director of the Home was **WILHELM DANTINE** (1911–1981), a war veteran who, like my father, had been called from his parish to serve in Hitler's army and experienced combat for long periods of time as an artillery gunner. The experience made him slightly deaf. He was

---

1. The allies decided that Austria was to be a neutral country after the war. But Russia blocked the move in the United Nations until 1955. In the meantime, the four military powers, the United States, England, France, and Russia, occupied the country. My residence was in Burgenland, a province southeast of Vienna in the Russian sector.

fifty, married with six children, ranging in age from infants to early teens. Since the children's mother was a full-time high school teacher, her mother helped raise the children in an apartment in the dormitory. They could be found almost everywhere in the house, noisy in their living and playing. Dantine was usually in his quiet study two floors down, working on his doctoral dissertation dealing with the interpretation of the Lord's Supper. He looked like a stout retired army officer, smooth-faced, with an aquiline nose; he walked like a horse, his face slightly nodding as if he were half asleep (as he often was!). His only formal duty was to conduct a brief compulsory morning worship service, always with a homily on the biblical lessons of the church year. After the service there was a community breakfast with a discussion of various issues pertaining to life within and outside the Home. Though working on his doctorate almost day and night, he always found time for serious dialogue and counsel. One could trace him by the smoke of his pipe or cigar. When I told him about my vocational uncertainties, he just said, "Check things out, use your head, and look for clues. But know that Christians are always nailed to one cross or another. The best theology is a 'theology of the cross,' an inconvenient way of life and thought." He had a reputation of cutting the knot of puzzling issues and coming straight to the point.

I pondered over these words and continued to share my reflections with Dantine. These reflections also dealt with the question of whether I wanted to become a parish pastor or a teaching theologian, tied to the church or only the academy. Dantine advised me to be patient and wait, reminding me of my confirmation epigram that "those who wait for the Lord" might also master vocational problems! After the first semester I felt certain that I wanted to work in the church, either in Austria or elsewhere. Dantine applauded my decision. I felt I had found a friend for life, fulfilling the role of "spiritual director" (a Roman Catholic designation, as I had learned from a fellow high school student who had become a seminarian).

Dantine and I became friends for life. I always saw him when I traveled many times to Vienna during my studies in Switzerland and from my new home in the United States. He received his doctorate, served as pastor of the "Student Congregation" (*Studentengemeinde*) in Vienna,[2] and became Professor of Systematic Theology there. He was a beloved pastor and exciting teacher, well known as a Lutheran, ecumenical theologian. My first difficult assignment as a vicar in Austria was made more bearable through his counseling; and I would not have immigrated to the United States without his approval. He also made it possible for me to become a member of the International Congress for Luther Research, and we both attended our first congress in Järvenpää, Finland in 1966. I translated his seminal study, *Justification of the Ungodly* (1968). During various ecumenical journeys Dantine dropped in for a brief visit in my home in Gettysburg, Pennsylvania.

Already during the first semester I saw a "clue," as Dantine had alerted me to expect; indeed, ran straight into it. It was a lecture given by **VIKTOR FRANKL** (1905–1997), a Jewish psychiatrist who had survived a concentration camp. The course he taught, Introduction to Psychology, focused on "the search for meaning" (the title of his bestselling book of 1959). He was forty-five, slender, bespectacled, and looked

---

2. Created after the war at many universities.

people in the eye when speaking or listening to them. Unlike other professors, he did not leave the classroom after the lecture but stayed to talk with students who crowded around him. I was fascinated by the way he talked about flashback memories as a means of survival imbedded in the conscious or subconscious mind. They might be of a religious nature or simply a wise saying about life. Frankl was credited with the creation of the "third Viennese school of psychotherapy," called "Logo-therapy" (from the Greek *logos*, "word"), after Sigmund Freud (1856–1939) who linked mental illness with sexual infancy and Alfred Adler (1870–1937) who traced mental illness to cultural and social factors. I had to talk to him. But first I headed to the university library to read his book *From Death Camp to Existentialism* (1946). Its original title was *Saying Yes to Life, in Spite of Everything: A Psychologist Experiences the Death Camp* (*Trotzdem Ja zum Leben sagen: Ein Psychologe erlebt das Konzentrationslager*, 1945). The book was published in English under the title, *Man's Search for Meaning: Introduction to Logotherapy*. I also picked up a book of his dealing with God, *The Unconscious God* (1948). The books echoed my own, much more modest, experience of survival. When I related this experience to him, he agreed to meet with me. After an intensive dialogue with him, I learned that countless interviews with survivors of all kinds of catastrophes, ranging from death camps to terminal illnesses, provided him with solid evidence that quick recall of a religious or wise saying made people survive as well, or even better, than specific drills, like boot camps for marines. I told him about my flashback in a life-threatening situation at age fourteen with Russian occupation soldiers when I crashed into a roadblock with my bicycle, slightly injuring a soldier. An officer interrogated me, mixed with some beating; he told me that I would be shot. While blindfolded and tied to a tree, another officer appeared, asking whether I was a gypsy (since I looked like one). I said, "Yes," because my father had had good relations with gypsies in his parish, buying berries and mushrooms from them. The gypsy families had been transported to a death camp during the war; a few survived and were well treated by the Russians. My quick answers in the gypsy dialect persuaded the officer to let me go. I grabbed my bike and ran until I collapsed. Part of my confirmation epigram about living in the presence of God without fainting flashed through my mind. It had given me the extra strength to survive, evidenced in a presence of mind generating the invention of a link with gypsies who, as victims of the Hitler regime, might invoke pity and mercy. While others might have collapsed *in* the face of death, I did so *after* the threat. Other, similar experiences later verified that I could be "cool" in difficult circumstances. I related my encounter with Frankl to Dantine. "There is your clue," he said. But he also warned me not to view it like a once-and-for-all conversion experience, as Pietists and Fundamentalists do, but as the first of other road signs on the trek of Christian life, especially in the ordained ministry. He called them "stations" and "sources for survival" during the interim between personal birth and death in the wider context of the time between Christ's first and second coming. "It's [the Christian life] all penultimate and cruciform," muttered Dantine,[3] half asleep in a cloud of smoke, sipping on his last glass of cognac around midnight. It dawned on me that Frankl's counsel to "search for meaning" was, in my

---

3. A play of words in German: *Alles ist vorletzt und verletzt*— "Everything is penultimate and hurt."

case, an anticipation of a never-ending future without evil, suffering, and death. His affirmation of an "unconscious God" meshed with my being conscious of "God in Christ" and of an ultimate existence with him, as confessed by the apostle Paul: "Now we see in a mirror dimly, but then we will see face to face" (1 Cor 13:12). Frankl alerted me to the search for meaning as survival power, evidenced as life-asserting conscious, unconscious, or subconscious convictions disclosed in flashbacks in life-threatening situations. Dantine linked these convictions with the minimal parental Christian catechesis of my childhood, mixed with Hitler Youth experiences.[4] I had become ready for a lifelong exploration of the meaning of hope as the power to endure the mean, meantime of earthly life—to "run without being weary, walk and not faint" (Isa 40:31). When Frankl was on a lecture tour in Gettysburg years later, I gratefully communicated to him how he, together with Dantine, helped to "make my day" as a teaching theologian and pastor.

There were two other memorable teachers in Vienna: Gustav Entz, Professor of Practical Theology, and Josef Bohatec, Professor of Reformed (Calvinist) Theology, representing the smaller portion of the Austrian Church of the Augsburg and Helvetic Confessions.[5] Although both were

4. Hitler Youth: a paramilitary youth organization of boys from ages ten to eighteen (similar to Boy Scouts), named after the German tyrannical ruler Adolf Hitler (1933–1945). The training stressed political ideology, sports, and war games.

5. The Augsburg Confession of 1530 became the accepted Lutheran norm, together with other documents, such as Martin Luther's catechisms. See *The Book of Concord: The Confessions of the Evangelical Lutheran Church*. The Helvetic Confessions (from *Helvetia*, the Latin name for Switzerland) of 1536 united the Reformed (Calvinistic) Protestants in Switzerland. Text in Schaff, *Creeds of Christendom* (1990), 1:388–420.

retired (emeriti) and in their seventies, they were called to fill assignments for which there was not yet an established faculty because of the difficult post-war years.

GUSTAV ENTZ (1884–1957) served as Dean pro tem when I matriculated. He was a native of Vienna with a long record as a pastor, teacher, and missionary in the city, organized as "inner (domestic) mission," (compared to "foreign mission"). A lifelong bachelor, known as "Papa Entz," he was always ready to communicate and exercise pastoral care. Tall, slender, with white hair, long beard, and always in a black suit with a white shirt and a bowtie, he was the most popular preacher in the city, known for his stories and opinions. He was the first professor I met, and experienced immediately his "impractical care," as I heard from other students. I was exposed to this care when "Papa Entz" encountered me coughing. He quickly advised me to do the "Kneipp Cure," using hot and cold-water baths, mixed with very cold wet towel flagellation.[6] Such and other idiosyncratic counseling verified the popular notion that Papa Entz was "professor of impractical theology!" The verification continued when I later enrolled in his class on preaching. Its main requirement was to hear Papa Entz preach at the largest Lutheran church in the city and then, on Monday, to analyze the sermon in class. My most memorable class was one dominated by a peculiar accident. When Papa Entz appeared on the pulpit, having climbed the dark hidden staircase leading to the sacristy, his forehead struck the rear

---

First edition published in 1877. See also "Helvetic Confessions" in *The Oxford Encyclopedia of the Reformation*, 2:219–22.

6. The treatment originated with the Bavarian priest Sebastian Kneipp (1821–1897) and became known worldwide well into the twentieth century.

wings of the large gold-plated iron bird on the roof of the pulpit; the bird was to symbolize the Holy Spirit hovering over the preacher. Entz had forgotten to duck as one of the tallest preachers in that church. Feeling the pain, he covered his forehead with the left arm and stepped backwards to the staircase. After a long minute, he appeared again and began his sermon, bravely enduring the swelling (without blood) of his left brow. When the class met on Monday, with Papa Entz's still visible swelling, he followed his established routine beginning with two questions: 1) "Was my sermon within the recommended length of twenty minutes?" and 2) "How would you rate it on a scale of 'very good,' 'average,' or 'weak'?" After a pause, one student, a veteran paratrooper honored for bravery in the war, got up and said in a very formal tone, "Professor Entz, this particular sermon was three minutes longer and quite swollen." The whole class chuckled. Papa Entz pulled his golden pocket watch from his vest, opened its cover, looked at it and said, "Indeed, it was too long. But it had its proper volume in its homiletic and theological construction." Everyone was relieved that he managed a personal offense so well. The clash between the head of Papa Entz and a wing of the Holy Spirit in Vienna became a lasting source of entertainment.

But there was a dark side of the friendly, caring Professor Entz. He was a committed National Socialist (Nazi) during the regime of Adolf Hitler and a radical lobbyist for the annexation of Austria to Germany in 1938. Moreover, he worked in a "scientific" institute for the propagation of anti-Semitism in Vienna and called on the church to purge itself from Jewish elements. Thus he supported the 1932 "Platform" of the Nazi faction of German Lutherans known as "German Christians" (*Deutsche Christen*).[7] Although he no longer pursued such activities after the war, he never denounced his political past and racist ideology. Perhaps he was too naive and childlike, known as a scholar for his Plato research and well liked as a pastor. When other students and I asked him about his opinion of Hitler, he said: "Well, Adolf Hitler was alright as a person. But as a 'Leader' (*Führer*) he was impossible." Comments like these, distinguishing between person and office, alerted me to the popular dangerous differentiation of private and public morality, often expressed by cautious minds in Austria and Germany in regard to the Jewish holocaust. Comments such as, "I minded my own business and stayed away from politics. Don't accuse me of anything. I never killed a Jew." I found some redeeming value in the fact that the Entz Foundation in Vienna was renamed "Dantine Foundation" after the death of "Papa Entz."

JOSEF BOHATEC (1876–1954) was a native Czech who was educated in Germany and became Professor of Reformed (Calvinist) Theology in Vienna beginning in 1913. He had become renowned through his voluminous work on Calvin, known best by his massive book *Calvin's Doctrine of State and Church* (German 1937). But when he came out of retirement he taught a course on the Gospel of John, one of the least profitable experiences in my graduate studies. Since it was the only course on the Bible in my first semester I enrolled in it. In a series of three lectures every week for a semester (about four months) Bohatec covered only the first 18 verses of chapter 1 ("The Word Became Flesh") because he became totally immersed in speculations about

---

7. English text in Littell, *The German Phoenix*, 180–83. The faction was opposed by the supporters of "The Barmen Declaration" of 1934, authored by Karl Barth and others. See ibid., 184–88.

the "Word" (*logos* in Greek). All of us students (a group of about twenty) agreed that Bohatec must have suffered from dementia, unable to pursue a systematic presentation of an assigned subject. He was always accompanied by his wife, said to be a woman of means who assisted him in everything he did. He was a small man with an untamed shock of grey hair, thick eyeglasses, and a goatee. In the lectures he could only be heard but not seen since he was too weak to stand behind the rostrum. But when he thought that something needed to be emphasized, he slowly raised his right hand and, when it was fully raised, he made his point, whose meaning, however, was missed by the hearers.

I had some conversations with him about the Austro-Hungarian Empire, our common political past since I often visited Hungary, the native land of my father, neighboring Czechoslovakia where Bohatec had grown up. But I could not discuss with him his fascinating work on Calvin or any other matter pertinent to my theological education. He was a living academic relic, as it were, reminding students of the solid German tradition of learning so evident in his publications.

I returned again to Vienna for another academic year (1953–54) after my first stay in the United States. I wanted to get ready for the first academic part of the examination for candidacy leading to ordination. The comprehensive examinations covered biblical studies, church history, systematic theology, and ethics. The theological focus was on the normative Lutheran Confessions in *The Book of Concord* (1580). A second, "practical" part covered preaching, catechesis, pastoral care, and worship, followed by a year as supervised vicar in a parish. I passed both examinations without difficulties, the first before I went to Yale, the second after my return in 1955; then I did my term as a vicar.

2

Zurich University

(1952)

ü

DANTINE NEGOTIATED FOR ME a grant from the Swiss Reformed Church to continue my studies at the Theological Faculty of the University of Zurich for the second semester of the academic year 1951–1952. He told me that I needed to have a rather "normal" academic experience after a year in Vienna. I wholeheartedly agreed!

Again, I had free room and board (with three meals a day!) in a dormitory, known as International House, under the direction of **EDUARD SCHWEIZER** (1913–2006), a Professor of New Testament. A native of Switzerland, he was a lively, slender, athletic man in his late thirties who loved family life (with a wife and four children), the New Testament, and the Swiss Alps. When I arrived at the House, he ran toward me with a big grin, shaking my hand and saying in a high-pitched voice, "Welcome" (in the Swiss German I never tried to speak, not to mention master it!).[1]

---

1. It was the traditional Swiss German greeting, phonetically spelled *Gruezi*, "greetings," or when groups meet, *Gruezi miteinand*, "greetings together." This dialect, together with French in the west and Italian in the south, are the official languages in the country. Zurich and Basel were in the Swiss German parts of the country.

A small group of international students lived in the House, most of them from Germany (at that time more from the Communist East rather than the West). I was the only Austrian in the group. After a week or so, Schweizer made me part of a team of students assigned to play volleyball with the family. At the end of the semester he persuaded every student in the House to do a one-day mountain tour with him near Zurich. Everyone joined in, and we hiked up and down a mountain with a nasty glacier. But only Schweizer was equipped to tackle it; he had the proper shoes, clothes, and a pickaxe. Having done a few such hikes in Austria, I was the only student dressed at least partly for the occasion, with mountain shoes and a wind jacket. Schweizer never warned anyone about the dangers of such an undertaking. When the time came to get down the mountain, he yelled, "Follow me!" With the pickaxe between his legs, he rushed down the glacier while the rest of the party tip-toed their way down; a student from Berlin, older than the rest, fell several times in his Sunday shoes and suit, luckily without getting hurt. Everybody chipped in to help him down. Schweizer led everyone back to the city, intoning a few songs, and discussing the theology of St. Paul. He was one of the youngest scholars to occupy a chair as Professor of New Testament at the University of Zurich. During his long tenure he became a world-class expert in New Testament studies, known for not leaving a jot of the ancient Greek text unturned in order to assess the true meaning of a passage.

When I stayed with Schweizer in the spring of 1952, he had continued his impressive publications with two studies that attracted my attention: *Community According to the New Testament* (*Gemeinde nach dem Neuen Testament*, 1949) and *Spirit and Community in the New Testament and Today* (*Geist und Gemeinde im Neuen Testament und heute*, 1952).[2] As a Lutheran in Austria, the question of the authority of church structures was raised at the First Vatican Council in 1870 that promulgated the dogma of papal infallibility, ascribing to the pope the authority to establish specific infallible teachings, such as the dogma of the bodily assumption (resurrection) of Mary. Schweizer contended, with persuasive evidence, that no one particular structure prevailed in the New Testament. When I talked with him about this important conclusion, he said that the authority of the Christian faith is established by an inner relationship with the power of Jesus and its exploration by more than one person. But it cannot be reduced to a rational formulation. "It may come through intensive prayer, or not at all," he mused with his enduring smile. As a pastor of a small Swiss congregation, he sought to generate faithful sermons by inviting people to help him prepare them in an informal study of the prescribed biblical texts, thus sharing his search for a normative meaning. He never gave up preaching, the major attraction in a Reformed worship service, be it in a small parish of a former student, or in the famous *Fraumünster* Cathedral in Zurich.

Schweizer was the only biblical scholar who thoroughly investigated the issue of ecclesiastical structure in the New Testament. It was the enduring issue of the relationship between movement and institution, between "spiritual gifts" (*charismata* in Greek) described in 1 Cor 12, and their structural organization for the sake of mission, described in Matt 16:18 as "congregation" or "assembly" (*ekklesia* in Greek). He confirmed what Dantine had taught me in Vienna, namely,

---

2. English edition *Church Order in the New Testament*, 1979.

that *all* of Christian life on earth is penultimate and imperfect; there are no human guarantees for salvation, or an infallible authority.

I also used Schweizer's practice of communal sermon preparation, organizing a small group of young members (close to my own age) in the parish where I served as a vicar for a year before continuing graduate studies in the United States.

I met Schweizer again years later during one of his lecture tours in the United States. He had become an icon in his field and a scholar always known for his thorough critical work and simple, joyous piety. He was always upbeat and cheerful. When once asked by curious readers of his works to describe him in historical-theological images, I felt compelled to call him a modern St. Francis with a doctorate in hermeneutics (the interpretation of literary texts). For he exhibited a childlike love of nature, especially mountains, and he radiated a scholarly love of the New Testament, particularly its testimony about Jesus.

Another memorable experience of my theological education in Zurich was the encounter with the renowned theologian **EMIL BRUNNER** (1889–1966). He was the best-known theologian in Europe and in the United States, a splendid lecturer and preacher, and a pastor fostering a deep devotion to God and the world. When I knew that I could spend a semester in Zurich, I immediately plowed through Brunner's magnum opus in progress, the first two volumes of a three-volume dogmatics, *The Christian Doctrine of God* (1946) and *The Christian Doctrine of Creation and Redemption* (1950).[3] His ethics was elaborated in *The Dive*

---

3. The third volume appeared in 1960 titled, *The Doctrine of the Church: Faith and the Final Consummation.*

Imperative (1937). I was ready to adopt Brunner's systematic theology and ethics as the kingpin of my theological education. With him on my side, I thought, the Vienna Theological Faculty would be impressed when they put me through the evaluation routine in my examination for the first degree as the prerequisite of ordination.

My first attendance of a Brunner lecture was quite an experience. It dealt with ecclesiology, the doctrine of the church, which belonged to the third part (or volume) of his systematic theology. Brunner's appearance at the rostrum at 7:15 a.m. made the audience rise, a European tradition similar to the opening of a court trial when the judge appears. Then he led the audience in a rousing, popular morning hymn, "Each Morning Brings us Fresh Outpoured the Loving Kindness of the Lord" (*All Morgen ist ganz frisch und neu*).[4] Brunner was a native of Switzerland, an elegant man, in his early sixties, of medium height, with short white hair, smooth-shaven, and speaking in a very precise, non-Swiss German. He easily shifted into it, or into English and French, when questions were asked in these languages. Questions could be asked in class, with great care, of course, since European lectures were not combined with such a method of teaching. But Brunner had been a guest professor at Princeton in 1938 and was said to have added this American feature to his style of teaching.

I also quickly learned that Brunner's theology had been sharply criticized by his early friend and teacher Karl Barth in Basel. He rejected Brunner's notion that the biblical notion of humans created in the "image of God" (Gen. 1:27) also created a human ability to cooperate with God

---

4. See *With One Voice: A Lutheran Resource for Worship*, no. 800.

in the salvation from sin. When Brunner summarized his position in cautious, careful ways in 1934 ("Nature and Grace"), Barth emotionally responded in a brief tract, *No!* (*Nein!,* 1934). But they both agreed that faith is not just a human "feeling" or consciousness, as nineteenth-century Protestant theologians had contended, based on the popular work of Friedrich Schleiermacher (1768–1834). Thus Barth, Brunner, and their disciples had become known as "dialectical" or "neo-orthodox" theologians because they denied a "liberal," "natural theology" in favor of the dialectical mystery of God's incarnation in Christ, the "orthodox" or "confessional" teaching of the Reformation. Moreover, "natural theology" became the basis for linking Christianity with the ideology of the Hitler regime in Germany. A large group of German Protestants (mostly Lutherans) supported Hitler and called themselves "German Christians" in 1932. A group called "the Confessing Church" (*Bekennende Kirche*) opposed them. Their stance was summarized in the "Barmen Declaration" of 1934. Karl Barth, who drafted the declaration, was dismissed from his teaching chair in Bonn a year later and returned to his native Switzerland. As a former Hitler Youth, I had read about the "*church* struggle" (*Kirchenkampf*) in Germany, but not about the conflict between Brunner and Barth. Brunner himself joked about it in his informal meetings with students. I heard him make the frequent play of words related to his name: "Brunner" is derived from "Brunnen" (German for "fountain"), and he counseled students to drink deeply from the pure water of the river Limmat in Zurich before it became polluted when it flowed into the Rhine in Basel where Barth was teaching. I also heard the popular comparison of the conflict as one between a whale and an elephant (without a choice of who would be one or the other).

I was lucky enough to join a group of American students in their regular meeting with Brunner at his house, or on the Zurich Lake. Brunner would swim with slow rhythmic breaststrokes and talk with those accompanying him like small fish. I decided to ask him a question about his skepticism about the institutional church, expressed in his most recent small book *The Misunderstanding of the Church* (1952). In it, he contended that there was a radical difference between the New Testament church and the institutional churches. I asked, "What should *we* do about it?" He swam to a spot where he could stand, followed by other students. He did a ten-minute mini-lecture about his views. Then he turned to me and said: "My generation did not do well in this matter [reviving the New Testament view]. You must do better!" I often remember this remark when ecclesiastical bureaucracy frustrates me.

Brunner left Zurich after my semester there and went to Japan where a tiny minority of Christians had founded the "No Church Movement." It has been said that Brunner may have found in this movement an embodiment of the kind of church he encountered in the New Testament. He taught at the Christian University in Tokyo for two years; then returned to Zurich. When he preached at the *Fraumünster* Cathedral, he, like Schweizer, filled the church; I had a hard time finding a seat when I did not come early. A few years later, I read a collection of his splendid sermons, *The Great Invitation* (1955). He, like Schweizer, was committed and able to make the fruits of his scholarly work tasty for Christians outside of academia.

There was an odd, yet fascinating part of my stay in Zurich: a brief encounter with the world-renowned, yet controversial, psychiatrist **CARL JUNG** (1875–1961). I had heard of him in Vienna as the founder of the school of "analytical psychology" which included an analysis of extraordinary experiences, ranging from dreams to visions to psychic encounters with the dead (parapsychology). My early youth with gypsy playmates and their families had introduced me to soothsaying, palmistry, magic tricks, and other phenomena; but I never became a "believer."

I read on the university bulletin board that the Carl Jung Institute in Küsnacht at the Zurich Lake offered a special seminar on an analysis of the experiences of psychic media. I rode my bicycle to the Institute, a beautiful, elegant two-story villa, with much green space around it, including large trees. Relying on my post-war teenage courage, I introduced myself to a secretary and asked whether I could briefly speak to Jung who was in the building. Mentioning my acquaintance with Viktor Frankl in Vienna may have helped. Jung appeared, shook my hand, and walked me to a parlor and, after a brief chat, told me to register as a visitor to the seminar on "Spiritualism." He was a slender, old man in his seventies, physically fit and mentally alert, with thinning white hair, a friendly bespectacled face with a small mustache, smoking a pipe and speaking German with a Swiss accent. When I mentioned my theological studies and admiration of Brunner, he smiled and said, "Oh, these theologians" (*Ach! Diese Theologen*)—not a complimentary comment!

I looked up brief, encyclopedic summaries of Jung's life and work, which in regard to religion, focused on the assumption that all religions, mystical experiences, visionary powers, and other similar phenomena are part of subconscious archetypes, such as "God." In addition, I also read Jung's most recent publication, *Answer to Job* (1952), which dealt with the question of why God would allow miserable things to happen to loyal Job. Not really answering the question, Jung used it to express his opinions on Christianity as a religion that is skeptical about subconscious mysteries, especially in its Protestant tradition. He expressed his preference for Roman Catholicism as a religion more open to the supernatural than "rationalist" Protestantism; he cited as evidence the recent papal infallible dogma of Mary's bodily assumption into heaven (1950).

The day I spent at the seminar on "Spiritualism" at the Jung Institute was fascinating, yet not very productive as an academic event. But it persuaded me that inexplicable psychological experiences exist beyond any doubt. I clearly saw and heard a medium write and speak Chinese without any contact, indeed any knowledge, about China. The medium was a simple Swiss peasant-woman who could hardly read or write, a fact verified by a very thorough background check. She spoke fluent Chinese and wrote full sentences in Chinese characters when in a trance, effected by recorded, hymn-like music in a darkened room with a small table light. Two Chinese scholars, who had been invited to observe the event, verified it as real and linguistically correct. Other staged experiments seemed less persuasive to me, such as a seance with an alleged contact with the dead. Reactions by invited scholars offered no satisfactory explanations or extraordinary insights. Jung himself linked the events to his notion of subconscious archetypes.

I was completely surprised and overcome with joy when Dantine informed me that my Swiss grant had been extended for a full academic year in Basel. "Karl Barth, here I come," I shouted inside my head! When I told Schweizer the good news, he asked, "What are you going to do in the summer?"—after the Zurich spring semester of 1952. I answered, "I need to get a job to make money." "Oh," he exclaimed, "I was just about to ask you about that. There is a small, but luxurious mountain hotel in Braunwald, near Glarus. I sometimes go there. The owner asked me whether I could recommend a student to work there for a summer." I responded, without any hesitation, "I am your man!" I made good Swiss money, increased in value through a profitable exchange rate with the Austrian currency.

3

Basel University

(1952–1953)

My grant for Basel freed me again from all expenses. There was even money for some books. So I could save my earnings from the summer. I was housed in a single room in the well-known and comfortable *Alumneum*, a sixteenth-century, modernized home for well-recommended male students of theology, with a preference for non-Swiss citizens. Again, I was the only Austrian there among about thirty residents, a majority from Germany, including some from the Communist East, and a sprinkling from other countries—France, The Netherlands, Scotland, Japan, and the United States.

The Director and "house father" was the well-known New Testament professor, **OSKAR CULLMANN** (1902–1999). His sister lived also there, nicknamed "Lulu" (from "Louise"), overseeing a small staff doing the cooking and housework. She was an old maid who always spoke French, even though she knew German. Cullmann was a German Lutheran lay theologian who liked to be formally introduced as professor where he taught in Basel, Paris, and Rome. The first two appointments were at the universities while the one in Rome was at the small Protestant (Waldensian)[1] Seminary where he only seldom taught. He was a very formal man, a fifty-year-old bachelor who never appeared relaxed in any company. Since his eyelids failed to uncover his eyes unless held up by special glasses, he created a strange impression when he approached anyone for a handshake because his head was bent back and the chin protruded. Almost bald, dressed in a comfortable expensive suit, he liked to talk about famous people he knew, such as the pope or members of noble families in Europe. I got the definite impression that he wanted to be liked and honored as a famous scholar. In this sense he was not the kind of "house father" I had found in Dantine and in Schweizer. But Cullmann did not seem to be chosen for the position to guide fledgling theologians but perhaps to provide a close encounter with a famous scholar. Be that as it may, there was good comradeship in the *Alumneum*, and I made a few friends for life.

Cullmann was not only well known as a scholar but also for his ecumenical engagement with Rome, advocating a thorough theological dialogue for unity between Catholics and Protestants. As an Austrian Lutheran I was quite surprised about such an endeavor and admired Cullmann for trying it. He developed good personal relations with members of the Roman Curia, including three popes, during his

---

1. A group named after Peter Waldo, a French critic of the church's worldliness in the twelfth century. Though persecuted by the Inquisition, they survived in the Alpine valleys of the borders between France, Switzerland, and Italy. In the nineteenth century, they were tolerated and became a Protestant denomination with about twenty thousand members, headquartered in Piedmont, Italy, with members in South and North America.

lifetime. I heard that Karl Barth, his colleague on the faculty, was quite skeptical about such a dialogue and, known for his satirical humor, had told Cullmann, "Your tombstone will have the inscription, 'He was the advisor of three popes.'"

I signed up for Cullmann's lectures on Romans and for a seminar on "Eschatology in the New Testament." I was disappointed about the way in which he taught: a monotonous style of reading from a text, and a hesitation, indeed anxiety, to have a lively discussion in the seminar with such an exciting topic. He also liked to quote himself: "As I said in my book ... " Besides, he was not much involved in discussions with his peers, other experts in the field who praised or questioned his pioneering New Testament studies. But while New Testament scholars, like Rudolf Bultmann,[2] concentrated on the existential impact of the gospel on individual lives, Cullmann focused on the notion of time as the interim between Christ's resurrection and second coming. Life in this interim makes believers aware of the difference between "already" and "not yet"—*already* with the Lord by faith but *not yet* by sight. I had read Cullmann's exciting book *Christ and Time* (1946)[3] in which he persuasively showed the difference between redemptive and chronological time. The book verified through an exegesis of New Testament texts what Dantine was talking about, though in different terms as a systematic theologian—the distinction, albeit not separation, between a "theology of the cross" and a "theology of glory." But Cullmann's writings did not come much alive in his teaching. I was tempted to tell him the opposite of what

2. 1884–1976. Best known for his controversial attempt to "demythologize" the New Testament. Details in his *Kerygma and Myth* (1961).

3. English edition *Christ and Time* (1950).

had been said to the legendary author of the *Compendium of Church History*, Karl Heussi: "I thought you were *not* a book."

But there were some lively moments with Cullmann outside the classroom, especially at the dinner table where he presided (eating a different, quite exquisite meal, than was served to the students, "for reasons of health"). Whenever a new student arrived, Cullmann asked him to introduce himself through a brief speech after dinner. He also had the custom of mentioning something or someone he knew in the home country of the student. One of the American students, a Texan, tried hard in very broken German, to describe the cattle ranch where he had grown up. "Many cows" (*viel Kuh*), "big horns" (*grosse Hörner*), "much, much oil" (*viel, viel Öl*); these words were the highlights of his speech which, of course, caused much laughter. When it was my turn, Cullmann said: "Welcome Mr. Gritsch. I had the pleasure of meeting the archduke of Tyrol, His Excellency [I forgot the name he mentioned]. Do you know him?" Of course, I did not and I could not care less whether I did or not. So I said, "I did not have an opportunity to meet Austrian nobility. All I know is that they are quite decadent." Right then and there, my speech joined the realm of the dead—but not without some smiling faces and even a chuckle or two as it is the case at peculiar funerals! I was also able to make some serious remarks about my home, my studies in Vienna, and my church.

We all tried to honor and entertain Cullmann in some ways: introducing him to visiting friends or relatives, asking for autographs, or listening to his tales about audiences as the ecumenical guest of cardinals and popes. A special occasion was the publication of his book while I was in Basel,

Peter: Disciple, Apostle, Martyr (1952, English 1953). We ordered a large, delicious chocolate cake from a famous pastry chef, with a white Latin inscription on the brown chocolate top, quoting Matt 16:18 (substituting "Oskar" for Peter): "*Tu es Oskar et super hanc petram aedificabo ecclesiam meam*"—"You are Oskar and on this rock I will build my church." Cullmann was pleased and invited his "student family" to taste the cake with coffee and tea. It was one way, among others, to liven up the tedious "prof."

I met Cullmann again two years later, in 1955, during my stay at Yale where he lectured on the Dead Sea Scrolls. But his reading of the English translation of a lecture in French could hardly be understood. Some of my fellow students asked me, "What did he mean when he spoke of the *boedi* of Christ?" I told them that he mispronounced the word "body." In 1968, I saw Cullmann the last time at the Ecumenical Institute in Strasbourg where he had stopped on his way from Jerusalem to Basel to tell of his successful efforts to create a center for biblical studies there. I was again impressed by this particular ecumenical effort to work for unity, especially between Catholics and Protestants. He had his assistant call me to his table where he held court, as it were, and he introduced me as one his "disciples" (*Schüler*), probably because I had begun to make my way in the academic world as a young "published" church historian. Books and papers kept coming from his study in Basel; former students published a commemoratory volume (*Festschrift*), and the World Council of Churches in Geneva honored his work in a memorial declaration after his death.

My real quality time in Basel was the encounter with the icon of the "dialectical," "neo-orthodox theology," **KARL BARTH** (1886–1968). When I attended his lectures for the first time, I immediately realized how different he was from Brunner, the polished theologian. I saw a professor in his late sixties, with a hawk-eyed, wrinkled face, large, thick eyeglasses, a shock of unkempt hair, a medium-sized, slightly bent but athletic figure, and dressed in clothes that seemed a size too large. I had difficulties understanding because his German was laced with a thick Swiss accent. It took me some time before I became adjusted to it and was able to appreciate his lively and clear presentations. In contrast to Brunner, his lectures were spiced with observations that were not in the manuscript. They were signaled by an exchange of spectacles, taking off the reading glasses and using another pair to see the audience better. Then he raised his right index finger, saying something like, "Well, one could use a much better way of putting it" (Ja, *man kann das doch viel besser sagen*); or, when annoyed about his critics, he declared, "Well, they might as well be Barthians" (the group he despised most since only Christ has disciples; earthly theologians use them for boasting and always need lessons in humility). Many quotations of Barth have been preserved, most of them marked by a self-critical humor. Transforming his lectures into a dogmatics, he anticipated its massive growth (fourteen volumes!). "I can see myself in heaven," he once said, "pulling a little cart with my dogmatics in it, and the Lord will say, 'Karl, that doesn't do you any good up here.'"[4] It was well known that Barth began each day with Mozart's music and a Bible meditation, working until midnight, except for some time for an evening dinner with close friends. It did not bother him that Mozart was more interested in Freemasonry[5] than in Jesus Christ. Barth

---

4. Mathonnet-VanderWell, "Interview with I. John Hesselink," para. 13.

5. A popular cult based on speculations about a nonpersonal deity known through inner illumination. Freemasons appeared in London,

found Mozart's joyful music to be heavenly. "It may be," he often declared, "that the angels go about their task of praising God by playing Bach. I am sure, however, that when they are 'en familie' [by themselves] they play Mozart." When asked to summarize his theology, Barth quoted a popular Sunday School song he learned from his mother" "Jesus loves me, this I know, for the Bible tells me so."[6]

I was quite taken by the contrast between Barth's childlike faith and his detailed argumentation from the history of Christian doctrine, the small printed parts of his massive *Church Dogmatics*. That is also one of the reasons why it became so voluminous. I discovered that most of the historical materials were collected from the work of students who had Barth as a "doctor father." It also was well known that his assistant of long standing, Charlotte von Kirschbaum, who lived with the Barth family, reworked seminar research papers and helped Barth in the collection of historical materials. I eventually learned that she was also quite involved in editing and typing the text of the *Church Dogmatics*. I attended the lectures dealing with the middle part, the doctrine of reconciliation. This attention to the link between systematic theology and church history helped me to decide to become a church historian who would have to live with the vicissitudes of time as a caveat against too

---

organized in secret Lodges in 1717. They quickly spread throughout Europe and were condemned by the Roman Catholic Church after they called for a "Counter-Council" against Vatican I in 1870, which established papal infallibility. Mozart's opera *The Magic Flute* has a Freemason libretto.

6. Quoted by Barth during his 1962 visit in Chicago. See Cameron, "Karl Barth the Preacher," 103. Also Online: http://www.theologicalstudies.org.uk/pdf/eq/barth_cameron.pdf.

much theological systematization. Theological systematization often causes unnecessary controversy provoked by the "fury of theologians" (*rabies theologorum*), a designation attributed to Philip Melanchthon, Martin Luther's friend and colleague.

A close friend in the *Alumneum*, Conrad Vogel, made it possible for me to visit the Barth home. Conrad's father, Heinrich Vogel, was Barth's close friend since the 1930s when they were members of the German "Confessing Church" that opposed the regime of Adolf Hitler. Vogel was a theologian and musician from Berlin; I came to know him better later. Whenever he visited Barth, they played Mozart. Conrad and I were asked to come for the music played by the trio of Vogel (piano), Barth and his wife (violin). The experience verified what I had heard about Barth's playing: it was more enthusiastic than skilled. Two aspects of my visit stand out: While listening to Mozart I saw a portrait gallery of theologians on the wall of the staircase leading to the second floor. I recognized Schleiermacher, the "father" of the liberal Protestant theology, rejected by Barth. But he honored Schleiermacher as a formidable theologian in his volume *The Protestant Theology in the Nineteenth Century* (1947).

Conrad also made it possible for me to "audit" (listen without active participation) one of Barth's seminars, which were always filled to capacity, mostly with his doctoral students. I was surprised about the topic, "The Theology of Alois Emanuel Biedermann (1819–1885)." Biedermann had been a professor in Zurich and represented a typical nineteenth-century theology based on Hegel and Schleiermacher. Why would Barth waste his time with a dead theological enemy? But I found an answer to this question after the seminar was over: Barth wanted to show his students that he could teach with great objectivity, elaborating with precision the centerpiece of Biedermann's work, his speculative Christology which had nothing in common with that of Barth. I was impressed to observe how a world-class theologian followed Christ's mandate, "Love your enemy" (Matt 5:44)!

During my year in Basel, it began to dawn on me that good theology should be grounded in the parish ministry; Barth was the most impressive model. His career developed from a call to a small parish into an intensive involvement in the theological and political world after World War I. The young Swiss pastor, despaired over his inability to preach the Word of God as interpreted by the liberal theology of his time, returned to the "strange, new world of the Bible"[7] through a very personal, powerful *Commentary on Romans* (1922) that shook the foundations of Protestantism. Barth compared it to a desperate grab for a rope that, however, was attached to church bells whose unexpected noise woke up the entire village. The ensuing theological debates made him write enough books, essays, and editorials to fill a small library. In contrast to other theological luminaries, Barth could only be encountered in his writing and teaching, not on lecture tours or in famous pulpits. He did only one lecture tour in the United States in his final years (1962), and he preached regularly only to prisoners at the small penitentiary in Basel. Mainline churches were much upset about his rejection of infant baptism, a view also shared by Emil

---

7. Barth used the phrase as the title of an address to Swiss pastors. Excerpts from the address are found in "Editorial: The Strange New World of the Bible," 412–16.

Brunner [8] and much debated by New Testament scholars, including Cullmann who defended it.

I saw Barth again in 1962 during my second year at Gettysburg while he was on a lecture tour. He had asked his hosts in Princeton to show him the famous battlefield of 1863, his historical hobby. His son Markus, a New Testament scholar at the Presbyterian Seminary in Pittsburgh, called me in Gettysburg to arrange an encounter with students at the seminary since, he said, his father's tour was confined to very formal appearances and he wanted to meet students. So I arranged a lunch at the seminary. Naturally, everyone who heard of Barth's visit to Gettysburg came, and the refectory of the seminary was packed with faculty and students. I greeted Barth when he stepped out of the Princeton car on a sunny May day in 1962. With him were his son Christopher, who taught Old Testament at the Ecumenical Institute in Djakarta, Indonesia, and Charlotte von Kirschbaum. As the only one who knew him, I was asked by the seminary president to welcome him when he stepped out of the chauffeured Princeton car. When I shook his hand, he looked at me and exclaimed, "Oh the Austrian from the Biedermann seminar!" He looked like an advertised tourist, attired in a green plaid sport jacket and a white shirt buttoned at the collar; two paperbacks on the Civil War stuck out from each of his coat pockets. After the brief welcome speeches, and the special lunch, Barth reached for his pipe. "Oh, smoking is not permitted in the refectory," said one of my colleagues at the table. "But we certainly can make an exception with our

---

8. Brunner in *Truth as Encounter* (1937) and Barth in an inflammatory lecture in 1943 and in *Church Dogmatics*, vol. 4, pt. 4. They contended that baptism should occur at a cognitive age. The debate was hampered by a lack of solid evidence for infant baptism in the New Testament.

guest," I quickly commented, pulled out my pipe, and turned to Barth. "Please try my Yale tobacco." My anxious colleague now nodded, signaling agreement. When the first puffs of smoke appeared above the table, another faculty member in the back of the refectory lit his pipe. Soon the entire refectory was blue with smoke! Barth rose to address the crowd. He said that he was surprised to find a Lutheran seminary on the Gettysburg battlefield; that he had an interest in the Civil War ever since he was given a set of blue and grey toy soldiers in his childhood; that he was not going to talk theology; and that he just wanted to see the sight where the actual soldiers fought. "It's good to be with Lutherans," he concluded and, with his right arm and index finger raised he asked, "You are not Missouri Lutherans, are you?" There was a spontaneous standing ovation, accompanied by two encores of "For He's a Jolly Good Fellow," and ending with my request for a picture in front of the Luther statue on campus. "Shall I kneel?" the honored guest asked, again grinning from ear to ear. Then the visitors left for the battlefield in Antietam, Maryland, where Barth insisted on firing a Southern rifle against a line of imaginary Yankee soldiers—with the special loud yell of the Confederate soldiers which they used when they attacked. I drove to Princeton for Barth's farewell lecture to an audience packed into the largest Presbyterian church. He agreed to answer questions submitted in writing while he spoke. Only one question was deliberately not answered: "Do you believe in hell?" Those who knew the finer point of Barth's theology surmised that he might not have wanted to get into the murky waters of a Christian "universalism" (the notion that everyone will be saved in the end, hinted in Col 1:20—in Christ "God was pleased to reconcile to himself all things"). He always viewed salvation as initiated only by God in Christ, without any "point of contact" (*Anknüpfungspunkt*) from the human side even though humans were created in the "image of God." He had made that clear in his angry "No!" to Brunner's contention that there is a positive relationship between human nature and divine grace. In this context, I recall Barth's humorous musing that the "trinity" in his family (son Christopher as the Old Testament expert, his brother Markus as the New Testament scholar, and "Father Karl" as the systematic theologian) offer the best God-talk, theology.

During Christmas break the Swiss Reformed Church invited me and a few other students to spend the time in Lugano, a small town on a beautiful lake and in the south with semi-tropical climate. I joined two other students from the *Alumneum*, a Japanese and a Dutchman, and seven pastors from East Germany in the comfortable retreat house on top of a hill flanked by palm trees and maintained by a female staff led by an excellent hostess. Among the pastors was the father of my friend Conrad, **HEINRICH VOGEL** (1902–1989). I was eager to get to know him better after the brief encounter in the Barth home. He had been a pastor of the anti-Nazi[9] "Confessing Church," became a close friend of Barth, and was imprisoned until the end of the war. Then he became Professor of Theology at the Humboldt University in Berlin. He was a stocky, jovial man, bald on top with lengthy thin hair on both sides of a large head, wearing thick glasses, and dressed in a suit with a vest showing a pocket watch on a golden chain. He was an accomplished pianist, hymn writer, and composer of chamber music. I had read two of

---

9. Abbreviation for "National Socialists" constituting the Hitler regime in Germany.

his books before going to Lugano, the most recent, *God in Christ* (*Gott in Christo*, 1951), a very Barth-like variation of Christology, and *The Crisis of the Beautiful* (*Die Krisis des Schönen*, 1931), a theological aesthetics, showing how music and the fine arts constitute a necessary part of Christian witness. He moved me later to include music in a catechism for adults.[10]

For two weeks I savored the elegant, yet informal, atmosphere of the house. All the residents received small Christmas gifts and were well treated with good food, local red wine, and the long thin (Brisago) cigars with a straw as a mouthpiece; Vogel liked being with us students, discussing our various experiences and theological interests. Every evening we had an informal evening prayer with Vogel playing the piano and leading in singing, including some of his own hymns. His survival as a pastor under conditions close to torture and his enduring sense of joy, expressed in music, made a great impression on me, confirming Viktor Frankl's work. The East German pastors, who endured less hardship than Vogel, were always serious and seemed to dislike Vogel's extrovert personality; they rarely participated in discussions and seemed to be busy with reading and writing. When Vogel staged a very noisy midnight celebration, using pots and pans from the kitchen as musical "instruments," his compatriots retreated to their rooms, accompanied by Vogel's noisy teacher-student quartet! I never encountered another theologian of aesthetics linked to Barth's unequivocal concentration on truly "good news."

After the Christmas vacation, I concentrated on Old Testament studies, offered by the well-known scholar

---

10. See Gritsch, *Handbook for Christian Life*.

Basel University

WALTHER EICHRODT (1890–1978), a native of Germany. He had published a three-volume monumental *Theology of the Old Testament* (1933–1939, English 1961) with the much-discussed view of the "covenant" as the uniting concept, extending to the New Testament. He also contended in an early publication, *The Sources of Genesis (Die Quellen der Genesis,* 1916), that the book of Genesis was a prologue to the Hebrew Bible rather than the first part of a sacred history. What was important for me was his scholarly answer regarding the controversial theological issue of the *unity* of the Bible. Unlike Cullmann, he was a committed member of the church. But his stance matched quite well with Cullmann's emphasis of the eschatological interim of the Christian life.

The odd man out, as it were, was **KARL JASPERS** (1883–1969), a German psychiatrist turned existentialist philosopher. Everyone in the *Alumneum* said that it was a "must" to see him. When I asked why, I was told, "Just go and see." So I went to a lecture on the history of modern philosophy, scheduled always at 3:00 p.m. Since there was a small crowd at the entrance to the building of the lecture hall, I added my curious presence. At precisely 3:00 p.m., a large black limousine-like taxi drove to the entrance. The uniformed driver got out, and, holding his cap in his left hand, parallel to his forehead, opened the back door. Bowing before the passenger with an outstretched hand, the tall passenger, dressed in an elegant black overcoat, his white-haired head covered with a black hat and carrying a black leather briefcase, put a banknote into the hand and proceeded to the lecture hall. It was the largest in the building, seating about one hundred and fifty. Sensing the atmosphere of an opera performance, I made my way into the hall. Well perfumed women in expensive fur coats, dominated my sight. I took one of the few empty wooden seats behind a writing table. Following tradition, everyone rose when Jaspers entered. He was a native of northern Germany, looking like a medieval nobleman in modern dress, every white hair in place, well fitting glasses on an aquiline nose. At precisely 3:15 p.m. (the arranged time for 3:00 p.m. lectures, granting fifteen minutes for going from one to another), Jaspers said in a well-sounding full voice, "Ladies and Gentlemen! Today, we continue with Soren Kierkegaard. My first point is this . . . " at 3:30, and at 3:45 he announced his second and third points, with concluding remarks at 3:55 p.m. I was fascinated by Jasper's pronunciation of the German "sch" sound: it sounds like the American "sh" when followed by a "t" (*Sturm*, "storm," is pronounced "shturm"); but in some regions of northern Germany it is pronounced "sturm" (like the "st" in English). The proverbial sentence is, *Ich Stolpere über einen Spitzen Stein*, "I stumble over a sharp stone"—"st" is pronounced "sht" and "sp" is pronounced "shp," but Jaspers pronounced it "st" and "sp." I could see some surprised looks in the audience, but no one dared to chuckle! Jaspers closed his lecture folio at 4:00 p.m., with a slight bow and proceeded to the waiting taxi, chauffeured by the same driver who had brought him to the university.

One of the Germans in the *Alumneum* enrolled in a Jaspers seminar on St. Augustine. He praised Jaspers as one of the best teachers he had had in his first two years of graduate studies. But this student was a mini-edition of Jaspers—almost as formal and vane as he! I do not recall the content of the lectures but only their form. Satirical critics called them "Jaspers show" a play of words on "Jasperle Theater" (*Kasperletheater*)—Punch and Judy Show. I tried to read Jaspers rather than hear him; two of his books were helpful, but not mind-changing: *The Origin and Goal of History* (*Vom Ursprung und Ziel der Geschichte* (1949, English 1953) and *Introduction to Philosophy* (*Einführung in die Philosophie* 1950, English 1951). Though renowned as an expert in medical pathology and as an agnostic philosopher, his teaching and the way he presented it was for me a most obvious move from the sublime to the ridiculous in academia.

4

Yale Divinity School
(1954–1955, 1957–1959)

SOON AFTER MY RETURN to Vienna, I saw an announcement of a scholarship for study in the United States. It was named after Senator William Fulbright who had sponsored a bill in 1946 to use the money from the sale of war surplus goods to finance an exchange of teachers and students between the United States and other countries. I applied for it and, after a very long application process, got it, due to my residence in the Russian sector of Austria. The grant was very generous: it offered free study for one academic year in one of three U.S. graduate schools of my choice, and it covered room, board, and expenses for books and travel. I was flabbergasted!

My three choices were, in the order of preference, Union Seminary in New York, the University of Chicago, and Yale University in New Haven, Connecticut. I was guided more by the lure of tourism than by the American values of theological education. Dantine and other advisors quoted a saying, familiar within professorial circles in Europe, "American stuff is not read" (*Americana non leguntur* in Latin, to make it sound less offensive!). With respect to theology, one could hear the adage, "Theology is produced in Germany, packaged in Britain, and exported to the United States." Be that as it may, I thought; I was looking forward to an exciting, extended visit to "the land of unlimited possibilities" (as emigrants were heard to say).

The anticipation of a year in America spurred my preparation for the academic examination at the end of the year in Vienna. The year in the United States would be a wonderful vacation without any obligation for hard academic work. Everything worked as planned. I easily passed the examination and took off by plane to London, and by boat from Southampton to New York.

After adjusting my British (and somewhat Elizabethan) English to American standards in a crash program at Duke University in Durham, South Carolina, before moving to Yale Divinity School, I felt ready to dive into a new academic culture. I was housed in a small dormitory with my own room and board at the refectory. Shortly after my arrival I was asked to meet an "academic advisor," a sudden change from the continental European university scene. The advisor was a young theologian, **CLAUDE WELCH** (1922–), who was Director of Graduate Studies at Yale Divinity School for the current year. When I entered his office, he shook my hand with a big smile. He was a medium-sized, muscular young man with short dark hair, a clean-shaven face, wearing glasses, and smoking a pipe. "Well, Mr. Gritsch,"[1] he said, "What would you like to do here at Yale after your exciting

---

1. The Yale custom of addressing faculty members with "Mr." was borrowed from the navy to avoid any faux pas regarding proper titles. "Prof. Dr.," for example, refers to a teacher who earned two graduate degrees, a doctorate and a "habilitation" (a second piece of research for appointment as "professor" at a continental European university).

time in Switzerland with Emil Brunner and Karl Barth?" "I will do what I hope is a minimal requirement of academic work since I want to see as much as possible of America," I responded with my usual disrespect for people who tried to impose requirements on me. Welch pointed to a file listing my studies during the past three years. "You encountered my hero, Karl Barth," he said, "And you read his history of Protestant theology in the nineteenth century. I am teaching a major course on that and work with students on special aspects in a seminar. I hope you will join us." Then he listed some of the big names in the joint faculties of the Divinity School and the University. "You can also easily commute to Union Seminary in New York and to Harvard," he remarked. "You could even earn a degree as a souvenir of your stay, a 'Master of Sacred Theology' (STM), by enrolling in four approved teaching events, with a written thesis of your choice."

I told him that I did have a particular interest generated by my examination topic in church history in Vienna: "The Theological Foundations of Thomas Müntzer's Revolutionary Program."[2] "Well," said Welch, "you are in the right place because Professor Roland Bainton's special interest is also in what he calls 'the left wing of the Reformation.' But why are you interested in this aspect of the Reformation? I thought as a Lutheran you might want to do Luther research with Bainton whose biography of Luther (*Here I Stand*, 1950) has become a bestseller." I told Welch that eventually

---

2. One of the most radical reformers in the sixteenth century, advocating the establishment of a theocracy through the Peasant Rebellion of 1525. Martin Luther viewed his execution as a just verdict for being in league with Satan. Centuries later, he was hailed as the true hero of the Reformation in Communist East Germany.

I wanted to concentrate on Luther, but with an approach from the "left wing" in order to view him first through the eyes of his Protestant enemies. I also shared with him my intention of becoming a church historian rather than a systematic theologian because systems tend to overlook or to underestimate the mysteries of faith. "Exactly my view!" Welch said, nodding his head. "That is why I am studying nineteenth-century Protestant theology. Otherwise, I could not do systematic theology today." Before I left, he indicated that he, too, was going to apply for a Fulbright scholarship to study with Karl Barth.[3]

Hindsight suggests that this conversation became another significant signpost on the road of my theological education. I quickly went to the library to read Welch's published Yale doctoral dissertation, *In this Name: The Doctrine of the Trinity in Contemporary Theology* (1952) and the biography of Martin Luther, *Here I Stand* (1950) by **ROLAND BAINTON** (1894–1984). I could not wait meeting the author! It was a memorable meeting in his office at the university library, decorated with stained glass windows and filled with books. Bainton was sixty, short, slightly built, with a shock of lengthy gray hair, dark-rimmed glasses, dressed in a simple suit, wearing a bowtie. "*Erich? Willkommen!*" he said in German with a strong American accent. Then we talked for more than an hour. Welch had called him to arrange the meeting. I congratulated Bainton on his Luther book and asked him why he combined his Luther research with a strong interest in the "left wing of the Reformation" (radical reformers, with Luther in the center and Catholics

3. He was a Fulbright Scholar in 1956–57 in Heidelberg Germany. His extensive work on nineteenth-century Protestant theology was published as *Protestant Thought in the Nineteenth Century*, 2 vols. (1972–85).

on the right).⁴ "Oh," he said, "They have been neglected even though some of them were proponents of religious liberty. I have sketched them as pioneers of later, more enlightened, times. I am a pacifist, my wife is a Quaker,⁵ and I like the Quaker theological tradition and support their work for people in need." When I told him of my study of Müntzer, he said: "This radical was probably the first Protestant theocrat. You should publish your findings."

Welch and Bainton had managed to change my mind: I decided to go for the STM program and boast about my first (American) degree in theological education! Running to and fro from one course or seminar to another, the assigned readings, and required papers made me look like an ambitious Ivy Leaguer! I signed up for Bainton's Survey of Church History and a seminar on "The Social Teachings of the Church."⁶ His lectures were performances, and students were said to have preferred them to going to a movie or

---

4. See Bainton, "The Left Wing of the Reformation," 124–34.

5. A nickname for "The Society of Friends," founded in England by George Fox who had a mystical conversion experience resulting in a repudiation of force, oaths, and war. The groups assembled for worship and "quaked" when feeling possessed by the Holy Spirit. Persecuted, many Quakers fled to America and became known through their intensive humanitarian efforts, especially their care for the hungry and victims of society. Bainton was ordained by Congregationalists, a group opposed to the Church of England in the sixteenth century; they are also known as "Independents" and "Separatists." There is a delightful autobiography of Bainton, *Roly: Chronicle of a Stubborn Non-Conformist* (1985). The book is only available for those who contribute to the Roland H. Bainton Fund, which brings to the school eminent spokespersons for his scholarly and moral causes.

6. The title of a massive study (1922) by the German scholar Ernst Troeltsch, who had renowned disciples in the United States, including Bainton and the brothers Reinhold and Richard Niebuhr.

other forms of entertainment. Bainton liked a stage. Every year, before the Christmas vacation, he appeared in the large lounge of the Divinity School (called "commons") as Martin Luther, preaching on the biblical story of Christmas. The place was packed with faculty and students, some of whom were seen rolling on the floor with laughter. I recall his dramatic chiding in his Luther exposition of the events in the manger: how much better care the audience would have provided than did the people of Bethlehem. People helped Christ neither then nor now. If they did, they would be out in the world helping Christ who comes in the suffering neighbor.[7]

The classroom became Bainton's stage, and his books read like novels. He may have been the only church historian who sold more than a million copies of his Luther biography. On the other hand, he seems to have adhered to the German distinction of "the history of the church" (*Kirchengeschichte*) and "the history of doctrine" (*Dogmengeschichte*). He focused on biography and institutional developments rather than theology. The lectures always had three sections, spiced with humor and, occasionally, with satire. I recall a formal guest lecture on Luther in Gettysburg, followed by questions from the audience. When a very tall, obese pastor stood up and asked with a droning voice, "Professor Bainton! Whatever happened to Luther's children?" Bainton responded, with an equally loud voice, "They all died." The roaring laughter and applause of about five hundred people could be heard in the street. Bainton also expressed his satirical humor in well-known cartoons, and many renowned visitors at Yale left

---

7. Bainton published his Luther sermons as *The Martin Luther Christmas Book: with Celebrated Woodcuts by His Contemporaries* (1948).

with uncomplimentary depictions of their personalities! The seminars engaged in solid research, governed by Bainton's well-known rules: to open with prayer, exclude smoking, and end on time. He "enforced" the first two rules by issuing ballots for a secret vote whose outcome was always predictable because no one dared to vote against praying and for smoking. But Bainton always graciously thanked the seminar members for their democratic action.

I had numerous meetings with Bainton regarding my STM thesis on Thomas Müntzer. He allowed me to submit it to him in German because of my tight academic schedule. With my "souvenir" (the STM degree) in my luggage, I left for Austria and eventually was assigned to be a vicar in a parish near Graz. It was part of my duties to teach all grades in the public school system in the town, ranging from elementary classes (age seven to ten) to the classical-secondary school, the *Gymnasium* (age ten to eighteen). Religious instruction, restricted to the two "state churches" (Roman Catholic and Lutheran-Reformed) was required unless parents and children opted out of it.[8] I soon discovered that teaching rather than pastoral work was my calling. But Protestants had little,

---

8. "State churches" in continental Europe were the result of church-state negotiations. They date back as far as 1555 when the Peace of Augsburg decreed that secular rulers determined the religion of their territory, with only two options, Lutheran or Catholic. After the Thirty Years' War, the Peace of Westphalia in 1648 added Anglicanism and Calvinism. The eighteenth-century European Enlightenment added religious toleration with negotiated rights for Christian churches. They were funded by taxes, with the option of being nonreligious. But a large majority of citizens opted for church membership, enjoying major passage-rites, such as baptism, confirmation, weddings, and funerals. A similar situation prevailed regarding religious instruction. Parents could decide for or against it for children under fourteen; older children could do so without parental consent.

Yale Divinity School

if any chance to teach their religion in a country with 94 percent Roman Catholics.

A peculiar incident made it possible for me to fulfill my desire to teach. In the middle of my year as a vicar, I had a surprise visit from a young Yale church historian, **SIDNEY AHLSTROM** (1919–1984). He had joined the Yale faculty when I was there in 1954. His field of research was religion in America. He fit the picture of the male American tourists I had encountered after the war in Vienna: a lanky figure, with a crew cut, a clean-shaven face, dressed in a shirt with a bowtie and a multi-colored jacket, not matched by the trousers, a cigarette in his mouth, and speaking with a drawl. We had talked about mutual experiences: he was a Lutheran with Scandinavian roots; he had been a Fulbright student in Strasbourg, France, and he had decided to become a church historian, focusing on the United States. I had taken his first survey course on American church history at Yale and was impressed by his sharp, critical observations regarding the origins and confusing spread of denominationalism.

When he saw me outside the church, he stopped and exclaimed, "My God, what in the world are you doing here?" "And what brings you here?" I countered. It was quite a coincidence, indeed, providence, for me. While at a conference of the Lutheran World Federation in Geneva, Switzerland, he was invited to visit a Lutheran minority church in Austria and was sent to my parish. After the weekend stay, he said to me, "Are you committed to this kind of ministry or do you still want to teach?" I told him about my dilemma—that it would be very difficult to teach in the public school system and indeed impossible to join the small Protestant faculty in Vienna. He asked, "Why don't you immigrate to the United States after your stint as a vicar, do a PhD with Bainton as your 'doctor father,' and find a teaching job in a college or graduate school?" After long discussions with my wife, family, and especially Dantine, the road sign pointed to Yale. Ahlstrom contacted Bainton and, after a few weeks, I was accepted as a doctoral student—with a scholarship covering fees, a paid position as an assistant to Bainton, and a job for my wife. Again, I was flabbergasted!

The next two years at Yale were dominated by an overtime working schedule mastering the requirements for the PhD degree in church history. Ahlstrom and I met again and became friends. When I asked him at the end of my stay at Yale, "What will be your magnum opus in American church history?" he quipped, "Oh, I am going to write the history from Betty [Elizabeth I in England] to Jackie [the spouse of John F. Kennedy who was rumored to run for the presidency]." He did! It was a book destined to become a classic study, *A Religious History of the American People* (1972).

My academic program brought me in close contact with other faculty members besides Welch, Bainton, and Ahlstrom. I encountered **RICHARD NIEBUHR** (1894–1962) as Director of Graduate Studies and as a renowned ethicist. In his early sixties, of medium height, slightly bent over, almost bald, wearing glasses, with a bony face, and speaking with a low voice while smoking a pipe, he seemed enigmatic. His book *Christ and Culture* (1951) had become the Bible, as it were, for an analysis of the dialectic between a sovereign God and historical relativity. I was more impressed by two of his other books, which I read for Ahlstrom's course on American Christianity, *The Social Sources of Denominationalism* (1929) and *The Kingdom of God in America* (1937). Meeting Niebuhr in person, I never expected to read his devastating critique of American

Christianity in a beautifully crafted sentence that I learned by heart and use to impress my audiences: "A God without wrath brought men without sin into a kingdom without judgment through the ministrations of a Christ without a cross."[9] What a difference between book and author!

As a teacher, Niebuhr demanded hard and careful work. The few doctoral students who survived his tough demands spread the caveat that one should do the PhD program with him only if one had the nerve and lots of time. My work with Bainton was fast, well organized, and reflected my own wisdom regarding doctoral work: "Getting a PhD is like getting a children's disease; the older you get the more dangerous it is." I somehow managed to get the degree after three years. A decisive factor was the theological focus of my dissertation, titled, "The Authority of the Inner Word: a theological study of Müntzer and other radical reformers." Bainton insisted that I should add other figures besides Müntzer since I was his only student to share an interest in the "left wing" of the Reformation. Niebuhr had only reluctantly agreed to let me arrange an unusually crowded work schedule in order to get the degree in just three years. "I do not think we should allow you to do this," he grunted through his teeth holding the pipe. I once again trusted my post-war persistence. "If I flunk one single requirement," I pleaded, "I will rearrange my program according to whatever cautious rules you apply." He approved what I proposed, and I negotiated with God every day to let me succeed and not be humiliated by Niebuhr! I proudly presented myself to him after my success, crowned with the acceptance of a job offer at Wellesley College (at that time known as the Harvard or Yale for women). My

---

9. Richard Niebuhr, *Kingdom of God*, 193.

good friend Leander Keck had taught there, and when he left he successfully recommended me. Niebuhr lowered his glasses, looked at me and said in a soft, disappointed tone: "But Mr. Gritsch, you should have come to me to get the best possible job. We have an excellent placement office at Yale. But you probably got one of the best at Wellesley."

Niebuhr was ordained in the Calvinist (Reformed) communion with a strong emphasis of a sense of the sovereignty of God without, however, being as radical as Barth, who rejected any notion of a point of contact between human nature and divine grace. He, like Bainton, was a disciple of the German historian Ernst Troeltsch. Warning against any idolizing of church and culture, he seemed to me to be close to Barth who openly criticized the praise of any culture, including the so-called "Free World" after the war with its capitalistic ideology.

My work on the dissertation and popular lectures on the history brought me in contact with the revered Professor **ROBERT CALHOUN** (1896–1983). He was a close friend of Bainton and a well-known ecumenist since his work with the World Council of Churches in Evanston, Illinois, in 1954. But at Yale he was a pedagogical icon: his lectures on the history of Christian doctrine had been taped and printed by students in three volumes in 1948. A lifelong (unpublished) Plato scholar, Calhoun transformed the lecture hall into a place of "living theology," as it were, guiding his listeners with incredible expertise through the puzzling, immense labyrinth of Christian thought—and without any notes, even when listing original texts on the blackboard! It was an amazing performance, yet without any attempt to be dramatic, as Bainton tried to be. Never before, nor since, have I experienced such a presentation of the history of

Christian doctrine. The Bainton-Calhoun ways of teaching have become my models.

Calhoun was a tall, friendly figure who reminded me of General Dwight D. Eisenhower, though with more hair and a more cheerful face. A tall man in his early sixties, dressed in a simple suit, and a light blue Oxford shirt with a buttoned down collar, Calhoun always smiled when he met someone—perhaps because he was hard of hearing. I noticed that he reached into his shirt pocket to turn on the hearing aid when I met him in his office. Bainton had sent me to him as a reader of my dissertation because it dealt with the doctrine of biblical authority. Calhoun reluctantly agreed, saying that Reformation theology was not his strong suit. I told him that listening to his lectures made such a comment irrelevant! He quickly became my second "doctor father." His observations and judgments were always right on target, and I saved much time not to have to discuss matters very long. His comment on a lecture of Paul Tillich at Harvard was quite to the point. "I told my wife afterwards that it was like taking a shower-bath: soothing and relaxing, but hardly necessary for survival." Such precise, indeed critical, judgment came from a kind, lovable academician who loved to grow roses and was known as "the egg man" by his neighbors because he occasionally presented them with a basket full of eggs from his beloved chickens.

I had heard that a historian, who fled from Nazi Germany, offered a seminar in the philosophy of history. I was unable to find such an offering, but Professor **HAJO HOLBORN** (1902–1969) offered one entitled, "From Thucydides (455–400 BCE) to Arnold Toynbee (1889–1975)." Thucydides had written a classic eyewitness account of the Peloponnesian War in which he fought on the Athenian side. The British historian Toynbee caused intensive controversy in his twelve volumes of *A Study of History*, contending that the continual clash of civilizations would bring the world to its knees. I had become interested in the German historian and philosopher Wilhelm Dilthey (1833–1911) who spent his life trying to establish the hermeneutical difference between "the science of the history of the human spirit" *(Geisteswissenschaft)* and "natural science" *(Naturwissenschaft)*. When I called Holborn's office for an appointment, a voice with a heavy German accent said, "Hallo! This is I. Who are you?" It was, of course, Holborn. My reference to Dilthey caused excitement in his voice. "Oh, he said, "you must come to my seminar on the philosophy of history next semester. I want students to choose a historian and work on his hermeneutics." Within a few days I was in his office in the Yale Sterling Library. Holborn rose from a chair behind his big desk, cluttered with papers and clouded with cigarette smoke from the strong brand "Camel," and shook my hand. He immediately offered me a cigarette (I smoked occasionally, but never a "Camel"). I accepted since his students told me that a refusal would diminish communications with him. In his middle fifties, he looked like an elegant German professor, with well-trimmed white hair, elegant glasses, clean-shaven, dressed in a three-piece suit with matching tie. But in his behavior he was lively, indeed excited, about his own work and about specific issues of research, talking with his hands and blowing a lot of smoke.

We talked for more than two hours about Dilthey, who was, as it turned out, Holborn's academic "hero." He told me to join the seminar because there may not be another student who could handle the large collection of writings (twelve volumes) and their complex German style; a native speaker would have an easier time with Dilthey. But I could select a topic like "Lived experience and rational understanding," focusing on hermeneutics proper. I agreed, of course, to work with him. I also asked him whether he would be willing to be one of my examiners in the "comprehensive examinations" before the writing of a doctoral thesis; I could choose the topic and method of one of six examinations, and I would choose Dilthey for an oral examination (quite a saving in preparation time, given my work in the seminar). Holborn agreed, complimenting me on my "wise" time schedule. Two years later, we had our dialogue about Dilthey, an easy "oral examination." Holborn was working on a three-volume history of modern Germany, which covered the time from the sixteenth–century Reformation to the end of World War II (1945), *A History of Modern Germany* (1959).

Another German visiting professor was **ERICH DINKLER** (1909–1981) who taught at Yale Divinity School when I was there for my doctoral studies. He was an icon in New Testament studies, working closely with the "existentialist school" linked to Rudolf Bultmann and his proposal to "demythologize" the New Testament. Dinkler was Professor at Heidelberg University where he also did research in early Christian art, assisted by his spouse Erika. He was a gregarious man who loved typical aspects of American life, ranging from football games to cocktail parties. Dressed in informal American clothes, such as sport jackets and various jeans, he went with students to ball games and parties, cautioned by his spouse not to overdo it, especially drinking and smoking. But students liked to offer him a cigarette and/or a drink. I signed up for his seminar on Paul's Letter to the Philippians in Greek. This language requirement limited attendance because only candidates for a doctorate in New Testament studies at Yale and Europe had to master ancient Greek.

The seminar sessions were often spiked with Dinkler's sharp wit, stories about war experiences, and specific interpretations of the text. The only other foreign student in the seminar was an older female student who had Dinkler as her "doctor father." She matched Dinkler's humor once with her translation of the saying of Jesus, "The spirit is willing but the flesh is weak" (Matt 26:41): "the ghost is willing, but the meat is weak"—using German words for "spirit" (*Geist*, "ghost") and "flesh" (*Fleisch*, food, like *Rindfleisch*, "beef"). A couple of weeks later, Dinkler also fell into a language trap when he said, turning to me as the Austrian in the seminar: "I am sure you recall the *siege of Vienna by the turkeys* in Vienna in 1529." He meant, of course, the *Turks*. I could not resist a satirical response: "I never heard of any siege by turkeys," I said. Everyone, including Dinkler, had a good laugh!

PART TWO

Excursions

"Don't Miss the Big Guns Over There!"

5

Union Seminary, New York

A NUMBER OF YALE students went to New York, either by car or by train (in about two hours) to hear lectures by two "big guns," Reinhold Niebuhr and Paul Tillich. I hitched a ride with three new friends, curious about the icon in radical American theology, **REINHOLD NIEBUHR** (1892–1971). As he entered the classroom for the course on Christian ethics, I saw a man in his sixties, tall, almost bald, with some hair on the sides of his head, wearing glasses, and reading most of the lecture in fast pace. When he stressed a point, his words were like bullets from a machine gun. His slight humor was heavily mixed with anger. In this sense, he embodied what he taught: a "Christian realism," angry about sinful human nature evident in American culture marked by political and social ills, ranging from tyranny to apathy. I found this attitude confirmed in his brief book, reflecting on the dire economic situation he experienced as a pastor (rooted in the German Reformed tradition) among autoworkers in Detroit. When he began teaching at Union Seminary in New York, he published a memoir entitled, *Leaflets from the Notebook of a Tamed Cynic* (1930). At that time, Niebuhr also met the young German theologian Dietrich Bonhoeffer at Union Seminary; he tried to persuade him, albeit unsuccessfully, to leave Hitler's Germany and become one of Niebuhr's colleagues.

I had begun reading Niebuhr's critique of American life in *The Tragedy of American History* (1952) and his magnum opus, *The Nature and Destiny of Man* (2 vols., 1941–43). His journal *Christianity and Crisis* attracted many dissatisfied church members, and his membership in the Socialist Party pitted his anger with that of his critics. My Yale friend James Holloway arranged a meeting with Niebuhr (Jim did doctoral studies with Richard Niebuhr). I was eager to discuss his sharp critique of Martin Luther, based on the criticism of Ernst Troeltsch, that Luther's moral teaching resulted in the demand for unconditional obedience to the state.[1] I pointed out that Luther clearly called for passive personal resistance and for active resistance if pope and emperor should unite and attack Lutherans in their territories.[2] Niebuhr listened and said, "I will compare your evidence with that of Troeltsch." I was tempted to remind him that he had in the past changed his mind, based on convincing evidence in regard to pacifism—he supported the war against Hitler. But I did not dare to mess with the icon of American theology!

Back in Europe, I read about Niebuhr's support of the Civil Rights Movement led by Martin Luther King and his opposition to the Vietnam War. My American friends told me that his consistent work of reform was finally recognized: W. 120th Street (the location of the seminary) in New York was named "Reinhold Niebuhr Place," and President Lyndon

1. Niebuhr called it a "curiously perverse morality . . . which encourages tyranny." See *Nature and Destiny of Man*, 2:194–95.

2. I published my findings later in the paper "Luther and Violence: a Reappraisal of a Neuralgic Theme," 37–55. Reprinted in *The Boy*, 227–58.

Union Seminary, New York

Johnson awarded him the Medal of Freedom in 1964. When I told Richard Niebuhr about the visit, he said, between puffs from his pipe, "Well, Mr. Gritsch, now you have met my brother." I surmised that he meant an obvious difference: Reinhold was an extrovert, indeed confrontational; Richard was an introvert, indeed reclusive. So they might not meet very often.

Niebuhr had visited Germany in 1933 (the beginning of Hitler's tyranny) and invited **PAUL TILLICH** (1886–1965), who publicly opposed the new regime, to join the Union Seminary faculty. Tillich did and became an icon in American academia. I attended a few of his lectures in systematic theology during my first stay at Yale. After he moved to Harvard in 1955, I met him several times in nearby Wellesley where I taught at the college.

Tillich attracted people as a wordsmith who forged catchy phrases, some of which appeared as book titles: "the courage to be," "the dynamics of faith," "the new being," "the ground of being" (God). Before I encountered Tillich in person, I read the first volume of his *Systematic Theology* (1951)[3] and *The Courage to Be* (1952). His "system" was elaborated in a much-debated "method of correlation," using categories of "being" (ontology) and of "existence" (existentialism). When confronted by problems of human existence, such as death, religion provides a solution, or an answer to existential questions—in the case of death "resurrection," through divine power. But Tillich used three sources for his method: the Bible, church history, and religion in various cultures. Thus the divine "answers" to the "questions" of human existence include non-Christian sources, religion in general.

3. Followed by two more volumes in 1963.

That is why the "method of correlation" generated intensive opposition on the part of traditional systematic theologians. Karl Barth, for example, called Tillich a "philosopher," not a "theologian." Consequently, Tillich's work was assigned to "philosophy" in German universities; he did not become an icon in his native country. Satirical minds linked his method of correlation to his relation with women. He was known as a womanizer. After his death his second wife published a memoir entitled, *From Time to Time* (1973), with juicy stories about *Paulus* (his first name in German) and his, often strange, sexual affairs. *Time* magazine reviewed the book in the context of an obituary entitled, "Paul Tillich, Lover."[4]

In his sixties, he looked like a successful businessman, perhaps a banker, in a business suit, wearing glasses, clean-shaven, with not very long, combed-out hair, and a sturdy body. He always spoke with a heavy German accent. During a lecture, a student who sat next to me and knew I spoke German asked in a whispering tone, "What does 'ambigu-eety' [phonetic spelling] mean? And what does he mean by it?" I said, "It is 'ambiguity' which means that one thing has more than one meaning. That is why Tillich uses the term all the time." After the lecture, we talked a bit about Tillich's "method of correlation" which ascribes two meanings to one entity, such as "God" and "ground of being."

I never clearly understood this Tillichian argumentation, even after some conversations at Wellesley where Tillich enjoyed formal and informal discussions with the women, both students and faculty. He shared his admiration for the German philosopher Friedrich von Schelling (1775–1854)

---

4. "Paul Tillich, Lover," http://www.time.com/time/magazine/article/0,9171,908007,00.html.

Union Seminary, New York

who moved from a focus on a dialectical thought process (as taught by Hegel) to a mystical view of the universe, presented in religious categories as indicators of an ultimate reality. He was also quite taken by the Romantic Movement, which moved students to view the revolution by Marxists and others in 1848 as a step to a better world. Existentialism, represented by the French philosopher Henri Bergson (1859–1941) and the Danish theologian Søren Kierkegaard (1813–1855), rejected such a view and affirmed the power of faith in the gospel, pointing to a new world after the rationalism of the European Enlightenment and faith in the moral progress of humankind.

Be that as it may, I was not attracted to Tillich then nor now; his thought process reminded me of a German cuckoo clock who makes this strange bird appear to indicate segments of time. Like the clock, Tillich seemed to be for the birds. But without the complex structure derived from nineteenth-century German philosophy, the preacher Tillich made a lot of sense, especially to anxious minds seeking serenity in a pluralistic world. He also had a sense of humor when flirting with an audience, preferably women. I recall how he entertained a group of Wellesley students, selected to have dinner with him and the faculty before his lecture. He pointed to his coat and said, "I have two versions of my lecture in my pocket, an easy one and a difficult one. Which one shall I use?" "The easier one," the students shouted in unison." "Oh," Tillich exclaimed, "I have only one version!" He sounded like a nice uncle who longed for admiration in close encounters with his nieces in addition to the distant respect he generated in books and lectures as the icon of Harvard.

6

Harvard

MY INTEREST IN THE radical sixteenth-century reformer Thomas Müntzer led me from Bainton at Yale to **GEORGE WILLIAMS** (1914–2000) at Harvard. During my doctoral studies, I read his English edition (with Angel M. Mergal) of a selection of *Anabaptist and Spiritual Writers* (1957). Williams viewed them as representatives of a "Radical Reformation" (called "left wing" by Bainton) in contrast to a "magisterial Reformation" represented by mainline reformers, such as Luther, Zwingli, and Calvin.[1]

Williams was raised and ordained as a Unitarian, but was respected, indeed admired, despite his unusual faith. When I met him, I saw a man in his late forties, dressed in a suit with vest and tie, his hair beginning to get white, with a clean-shaven, rosy-cheeked face, very professorial, polite, and quickly engaged in professional dialogue. Since he had spent several years in Europe, we talked about his and my impressions about studies abroad. One of his students had told me that Williams was feared in comprehensive doctoral examination because he would ask questions about minute details. Our conversation reflected that because he asked me

---

1. Williams derived "magisterial" from "magistrate," a reformation supported by princes or the state. "Radical" means the opposite, at times a revolution against the state.

how many casualties there were on the side of the feudal landlords in the final battle between the rebelling peasants and the princes who massacred them and had Müntzer beheaded. I happened to know that the princes lost only six men. Williams then talked about his extensive detailed work on a history of the "Radical Reformation." Since he liked to divide his findings into three types, I could not help joking and told him that he seemed to be quite "trinitarian" in his research but not in his theology. He took the joke quite well! He published a big volume in 1962, when I was beginning my work in Gettysburg. *The Radical Reformation*, as it was called, appeared in a third edition in 1992 (with 1516 pages!).

I met Williams now and then throughout my career as a church historian. The gentle, polite, and kind Harvard professor was found among the young American radicals who demonstrated for civil rights with Martin Luther King and against the Vietnam War in the 1960s. Williams outdid some of the demonstrators when he burned draft cards on a pulpit in Cambridge. We spent some time together at a meeting of the International Congress for Luther Research where he did a paper on "Luther and the Radicals." He did not want to say anything that was not solidly nailed down regarding this much-discussed topic. So he called on a few of us who knew the details of Luther's critique as well as the arguments of radicals against him. Williams did not like debates, especially not when all available evidence of the subject matter had not yet been collected. He never drove a car and spent most of his days in archives and libraries.

He told me that while he did research about Polish Unitarians, he met the archbishop Karol Jozef Wojtyla and predicted that he would become pope, as he indeed did in

1978. He, the Unitarian, liked the new man in Rome and published his findings in *The Mind of John Paul II: His Thought and Action* (1981). When I, as a member of the North American Lutheran-Catholic Dialogue, attended the big rally at the stadium of the University of South Carolina in Columbia, South Carolina in 1987, staged to honor the pope during his visit to the United States, I saw Williams among the dignitaries on the rostrum from which John Paul II was to address the crowd. The program announced that the dignitaries, invited by the pope to be with him on the rostrum, would say a prayer. "What in the world will George's prayer be?" I almost said out loud to myself. When his turn came, Williams, in his flowing red Harvard gown, moved to the microphone, bowed his head, and with hands clasped, prayed a beautiful prayer, lifting up the ideals of "wilderness and paradise" in a world too busy to meditate and to praise God for the gifts of life, especially the world of animals and plants.[2] He told me later in a phone conversation that he and the pope had become friends. A medieval pope would have ordered him to be burned at the stake for denying the dogma of the Trinity.

A totally different theological educator, but not a faculty member at Harvard, was **HENRY HORN** (1913–2007), the Lutheran pastor of the campus congregation known as University Lutheran Church (Unilu). I met him briefly during my visit from Yale and got to know him well as my pastor when I joined the congregation while teaching at Wellesley.

Horn met people with a smile and a peculiar handshake—there was hair on the palms of his hands! Tall,

---

2. The prayer reflected Williams' concerns described in his book *Wilderness and Paradise in Christian Thought* (1962).

sturdy, always with a clerical collar in a business suit, wearing glasses, clean-shaven, and smiling, he immediately connected with people, perhaps because he was the father of ten children who needed much friendly attention. Close to each other in age, they reminded me of organ pipes when they in their various sizes filed in with their mother into the first two pews in the sanctuary every Sunday morning. Horn was a liturgical scholar and a very effective preacher. No new Lutheran hymnal was published without his work and approval. Moreover, he was a very respected churchman who helped to shape church polity among the variety of Lutherans. He was a living part of Lutheran history.[3]

Meeting Horn in a conversation, one became instantly aware of his passion to push the minds of church members from a convenient status quo into the trials and tribulations of the world, the goal of solid education. He read the latest scientific achievements and daily news events. I heard one of his sermons that illustrated his call to stand on tiptoes so that one can see and discover a world beyond the status quo. The sermon interpreted Isa 25:6 (how God will stage a feast "for all people" with rich food and good wine) and focused on the bone marrow as a mouth-watering delicacy. He described in detail how his mother carefully separated the soft marrow from the hard walls inside the bone, then carefully placed it on a piece of toast and divided it into equal parts for the children at the Sunday dinner table. Horn's account of laboring for the marrow and of enjoying its taste became a simile of how Christians should reach out for life in the world.

---

3. After his death, a memoir with selected writings was published, *Hornucopia* (2008).

Horn decisively helped me to decide where I should start my career as a church historian. I did not want to stay at a college but to teach at a graduate school. It so happened that after my first two years at Wellesley I had an opportunity to interview for a position at two different schools. My Yale friend, Leander Keck, had arranged one at Vanderbilt University, and Bainton recommended me for one at Gettysburg Seminary when a faculty member asked him about Lutheran candidates. Since Horn was the best source for anything one wanted to know about American Lutheranism, I turned to him. As a graduate of Philadelphia Lutheran Seminary, with its reputation of being much better than Gettysburg, he suggested that Vanderbilt might be the better choice. But just as we deliberated about my future, Gettysburg announced the appointment of a new president, Donald Heiges, a graduate of Gettysburg and Dean at the Chicago Seminary. He announced his intention of introducing radical changes, aiming for excellence in academic and spiritual formation. The news changed Horn's mind. "You must go to Gettysburg," he said, "because it needs faculty members who are not Gettysburg graduates. Their academic inbreeding must be stopped, and Heiges will do it." Horn was right, and I moved to Gettysburg for a long career.

During my first encounter with Horn, he introduced me to a New Testament scholar at Harvard Divinity School, **KRISTER STENDAHL** (1921–2008), a Lutheran from Sweden. He had a personality that stood out in almost any group of people: tall, with a bony head, the hair combed down to the forehead, small eye glasses, always in clerical collar, dressed in a formal suit, and speaking with a heavy Swedish accent. He moved almost like a robot because of an enduring, incurable, painful arthritis. He was interested in my Basel experience with Cullmann whom Stendahl never met; but he had heard of Cullmann's ecumenical efforts besides his New Testament work.

After my first brief encounter with Stendahl, I read his published dissertation, *The School of St. Matthew, and Its Use of the Old Testament* (1954). In it, Stendahl showed his enduring interest in Christian-Jewish relations, which exclude any Christian mission to the Jews. My own reading of Romans 9–11 brought me to the same conclusion. But Stendahl clearly elaborated it, especially in his later thought and life. After my move to Gettysburg, I learned that Stendahl had made headlines with his lecture at the annual meeting of the American Psychology Association in 1961, "The Apostle Paul and the Introspective Conscience of the West."[4] He contended that Augustine, Luther, and other "fathers of the church" were wrong in their interpretation of the "law" as "disciplinarian" (Gal 3:24): its main function is not to bring sinners to repentance, thus creating a guilty conscience, but to lead Israel to a final union with Gentiles, namely Christians. The debate of Stendahl's lecture always flares up. I side with him and his biblical evidence, but also because the notion of guilt has been over-emphasized ever since Sigmund Freud linked it to anxiety as an inevitable part of human existence. Lutherans, in particular, have lifted up the "penitential struggle" (*Busskampf*, as Pietists called it) as a condition for salvation, almost drowning out the joy of being "justified by faith alone." Stendahl certainly knew the joyless underside of German and Scandinavian Lutheranism.

---

4. Published in *The Harvard Theological Review* (1963) and in *Paul Among the Jews and Gentiles, and Other Essays* (1977).

Stendahl was indefatigable in his work for the unity of humankind. Instead of prejudice, fear, or just polite distance, one should show a "holy envy," Stendahl advised, because one can always find admirable features in others, and one should desire them as building blocks for unity. Whenever I met him again, also as lecturer in Gettysburg, his arthritis had taken its toll, impeding movement and increasing pain. But when Stendahl began to speak I was immediately reminded of my confirmation epigram about the miraculous strength given to those "who wait for the Lord." He showed me the rare commodity of serenity in academia and in the church.

PART THREE

Teaching

"From College Girls to Seminarians."

7

Wellesley College

(1959–1961)

MY YALE FRIEND LEANDER Keck arranged an interview for a teaching position at Wellesley College, the "Harvard for women," recommending that I take his position after he joined the faculty of Vanderbilt Divinity School in Nashville, Tennessee. I agreed, even though I would be teaching a Bible course with other faculty members rather than church history. But Keck urged me to go to Wellesley and do what he did, namely, to use it as a base from which to move to a graduate school with the special field of church history.

I had anticipated to be interviewed by a woman. But the Chairman of the Department of Religion was a man, **FRED DENBEAUX** (1915–1995). An interesting image came to my mind when I met him—"an elegant football coach": tall, big, sophisticated, with a neat mustache, well-framed glasses, and dressed in a neat sporty combination of jacket and trousers. During our lengthy conversation, "Fred" (as he wished to be addressed) described my teaching obligations, a section of "Introduction to the Bible" (a sophomore requirement taught by the whole department), and an elective of my choice approved by Fred. He was quite interested in my European background and immediately approved my request to teach an elective course in Philosophy of History since it would blend with his elective, a History of Christian Thought. We ended the "interview" with a trip to a lavatory and, while we did "our business," he asked, "Do you want the job?" "Oh, yes," I responded. "It's yours," he said. "I will get the approval of the president, Miss Clapp, and do the necessary paperwork." I was tempted to ask why the only male chairperson of a department was so entrusted with power in an administration run by women. But I learned that he had created the most successful department at the college. It had the largest number of "majors," with the English department a close second.

I learned from Fred how to develop teaching tools, such as syllabi, student papers, examinations, and other pedagogical features indigenous in the "new world"; but I did not adopt his personalized view of church history. I will never forget the shortest faculty meeting in almost four decades of teaching. Fred called an "emergency meeting." Everyone rushed to the meeting, curious about the emergency. After a few minutes, Fred rose from his chair, raised his right hand and, using his index finger like a father scolding his children, he said in a somber voice, "We lost a Bible major to the English department. Go and teach like hell! Meeting adjourned."

The students respected Fred, indeed adored him as a teacher of the History of Christian Thought; fondly labeled, "the history of Denbeaux's thought." The secret of Fred's teaching was a dialectic of destructive and reconstructive analysis. A number of students said, "Denbeaux shreds what I learned to believe, and then teaches me what I ought to believe based on historical facts." Denbeaux deliberately taught "the art of Christian doubt," the title of the only book he published (1961). This "art" was a philosophical skepticism based on Fred's hero in classical Greek antiquity, Pyrrho (270–365 BCE). Pyrrhonism taught that happiness is based on suspending judgment because certainty of knowledge is impossible. Fred and I discussed and compared this ancient philosophical insight with the biblical view of all earthly thought and life as penultimate in the face of the biblical promise of a new, never-ending life with God in Christ. Mindful of Karl Barth and the normative Lutheran Confessions, I defended a stance based on the certainty of faith in Christ as a "Word" handed on by oral communication (preaching and teaching) and sacramental enactment (baptism and Lord's Supper). Since Fred leaned towards the Anglican tradition, we had much in common. His philosophical skepticism and my historical relativism were not too far apart. Besides, Fred disliked agreeing with anyone! When I read his book shortly after my move to Gettysburg, I called to congratulate him on his birth as an author. He became an icon at Wellesley.

8

Gettysburg Lutheran Seminary

(1961–1994)

D*antine in Vienna*, Bainton at Yale, and Horn at Harvard agreed that I should teach at the oldest American Lutheran seminary, given my predilection for working as a church historian in the field of Reformation studies with an eye on Lutheranism. Moreover, Gettysburg was poised to change with a new administration and new faculty members.

After a brief visit for an interview, I was called to a position on a tenure track. On the evening of the day of my arrival I was visited by **ABDEL ROSS WENTZ** (1883–1976), the retired president of the seminary and renowned church historian; he had published the widely used textbook *A Basic History of Lutheranism in America* (1955). He also had been a mover and shaker in the ecumenical movement after World War II. His son, who had succeeded him on the faculty, soon left for another position; he has written a biography of his father.[1]

---

1. F. Wentz, *Expanding Horizons for America's Lutherans: The Story of Abdel Ross Wentz* (2009).

Wentz looked like a businessman, short, well-dressed, clean-shaven, and used to being respected in a room with others he quickly dominated. It became obvious that he tried to tell me what to do in my work at the seminary and how to do it. Horn had forewarned me about him as someone who wants to have it all his way; but he also praised him as the honored "Mr. Lutheran" in America since he had dedicated a long career to the exploration of the Lutheran tradition in America and had introduced its power in ecumenism in connection with European Lutheranism. When we sat down for a conversation, Wentz first described his work in Europe, especially with German Lutheran leaders. Then he advised me to work closely with his son Frederick and to use a specific German bookseller to order books for the library and myself. I tried to match his imposing narration of his close work and friendship with renowned European churchmen and theologians by dropping the names of "big guns" I had come to know, but mostly non-Lutherans, such as Barth, Brunner, Cullmann, and others. I closed my side of the "argument" by comparing his and my status at the seminary. "Professor Wentz," I said, "do you enjoy retirement?" "Oh, yes," he responded with a smile. "I have now enough time to play tennis." "Since you are retired," I said, "you no longer have the formal call of the church to be responsible for the well-being of the seminary. I have such a call and will do my very best for the seminary in my work as a church historian. I hope that I can get your good advice now and then." "Oh, by all means," Wentz replied, rising from the chair, signaling the end of his "inspection visit." The visit was the beginning of a good relationship with "Mr. Lutheran" who was my living source for much information about Lutheranism in America.

The drive to revive the old glory of the seminary and put it again on the map of theological education brought the rising star of Lutheran theology in America to Gettysburg, **ROBERT JENSON** (1930–), known as "Jens" among colleagues and friends. His outward appearance was impressive: a man of medium height, well-dressed, often with a clerical collar, shoulder-long hair, a neatly trimmed beard, glasses, often wearing a hat, and sometimes walking with a cane (a decoration rather than a medical necessity). One could easily mistake him for an Anglican or Orthodox cleric—but one who played a mean trombone when motivated by a friendly crowd! As a close colleague for twenty years and a friend after he left the seminary faculty, I learned much from him, a student of Barth, with a commitment to Lutheranism. He did his doctoral dissertation on Barth's view of divine election, published with the blessing of Barth, *Alpha and Omega: A Study in the Theology of Karl Barth* (1963). I totally agreed with him that there is an enduring tension, indeed a life-and-death struggle, between the Christian gospel and religion, especially in the United States where a religious pluralism has polluted Christianity. Jenson also stressed the link between theology and worship. He composed portions of the liturgy for a new Lutheran hymnal and loved to preside at services. It dawned on me that the Lutheran "chief article of faith," "justification," signaling unconditional salvation through the "gospel," includes celebration because it is tied to "word and sacrament" in the Lutheran Confessions collected in *The Book of Concord* (1580). The doctrine of "justification by faith" can be sung, as Luther did in one his hymns.[2]

---

2. "Dear Christians One and All." A lengthy hymn, describing a dia-

While we both elaborated and taught the doctrine of justification in the required course on the Lutheran Confessions, we decided to publish our historical-theological work with students, in a book titled, *Lutheranism: The Theological Movement and its Confessional Writings* (1976), destined to become a widely used textbook. I also adopted Jenson's striking definition of Lutheran ethics as "the secularization of morality" (over against the Roman Catholic elaboration of an ecclesiastical morality in Canon Law). In innumerable discussions, accompanied by good food and wine, I cherished Jenson's critical reflections. We both debated our way through issues, ranging from "secular" ones (like the war in Vietnam) to "churchly" ones (like infant communion). While I imbibed systematic theology, he read much Luther, resulting in a number of lectures at the seminary's Institute for Luther Studies, which I had been asked to direct. My proudest moment in our relationship was Jenson's reluctant agreement to lecture on the notion of evil—a topic hardly ever well tackled by systematic theologians, especially disciples of Barth. Jenson's lecture, titled "Evil as Person," is a theological gem, focusing on God and the devil in the context of humor and death. Jenson contends that the devil is not a person and consequently cannot laugh about himself; he can only experience *Schadenfreude*—pleasure derived from the misfortune of others, and everyone hates him for it; death is the last of his jokes; but God takes even that pleasure from him through the resurrection of Jesus.[3]

---

logue between God and his Son on how to save the world. See *Lutheran Book of Worship*, no. 299.

3. Jenson's "Evil as Person" lecture is available in Gritsch, *Encounters with Luther,* 4:182–91.

Jenson summarized his work in two volumes of a *Systematic Theology* (2001). He taught others and me that theology by definition never ends. So he, encouraged and assisted by his spouse Blanche, has created a Jenson library of books, essays, biblical commentaries, theological conversations with his granddaughter, and even a play based on Ezekiel. When students created a group called "Seminary Players," Jenson directed plays, favoring the work of the Swedish novelist and playwright Johan Strindberg. The seminary library has a treasured short play, put on video by students, entitled, "Who Killed RJ?" (a parody of the TV series "Who killed JR?"). It describes a successful plot to kill Jenson. Evidence suggests specific suspects: I head the list because I do not want to share the royalties from the sale of our book *Lutheranism*. Among the other chief suspects is the head of campus landscaping; he hates Jenson for planting a vegetable garden at his residence on campus, thus impeding the fast mowing of grass by a tractor. Jenson's dead body is found lying at the entrance to the seminary chapel, wearing a hat and holding an umbrella. A faculty member discovers the body and attempts to revive him by reading a passage from Paul Tillich's *Systematic Theology*. After a few minutes, Jenson slowly raises his umbrella and exclaims, "This is bullshit!" Resurrected, he is surrounded by a frolicking crowd.

He enriched my historical work with his theological reflections. I still learn from him.

The new spirit of the seminary also brought much stimulation from the outside with teaching events for clergy and lectures. The new curriculum required an "internship" before ordination. It consisted of three months of "clinical" experience (work in a hospital, prison, or other therapeutic institutions) and nine months in a parish supervised by the pastor. The internship had to be done in the third year of the four-year seminary education. In the early 1970s, work in a hospice became a popular internship experience because of a bestselling book by the psychiatrist **ELIZABETH KÜBLER-ROSS** (1926–2004), *On Death and Dying* (1969). When she came for a lecture and seminar, she made me think about death, just as Frankl had alerted me to think about the meaning of life. I had an extensive discussion with her. A native of Switzerland, she immigrated through marriage to the United States and joined a growing hospice movement, involving seminarians in the care for the dying. She looked like a tough mountain climber, wore no make-up, and spoke with a heavy Swiss accent. In her lecture, she described five psychological stages of dying, based on what she called "scientific observation": denial, anger, bargaining, despair, and acceptance. I told her that these five stages echoed my own fear of dying when I was a fourteen-year-old soldier trained by German storm troopers to kill invading Russians. I asked her whether the fear of dying in a foxhole would evoke the same psychological reactions as did the verdict of death in a hospital. "I could feel anger and despair," I told her, "but not the other three emotions." She said, "That may be so. But my patients go through intensive counseling, ending in 'acceptance.'" She told me that she had begun work with dying children who communicated their image of death through drawings (often depicting cruel weapons like tanks). I still encountered her as an atheist. But I read later that in her final years she abandoned atheism in favor of a belief system that accepted "out-of-body" experiences and faith in the migration of souls. The encounter with her led me to a proposal for "death education" as part of parish catechesis;

some of my students did develop such a program, using the five stages of Kübler-Ross, combined with legal aspects such as making one's will and arranging one's funeral.

Another visitor on campus was the German theologian **JÜRGEN MOLTMANN** (1926–). I anticipated much from the visit because his name was linked to Ernst Bloch (1885–1977), a famous German Marxist Socialist who had written a biography of Thomas Müntzer "as a theologian of revolution" (only available in German, *Thomas Müntzer als Theologe der Revolution*, 1921); I disagreed with him in my book *Reformer without a Church: The Life and Thought of Thomas Müntzer, 1488?–1525* (1968) because he neglected to elaborate the theological reasons of Müntzer's radical actions. Moltmann had acknowledged Bloch's decisive influence in his popular book *The Theology of Hope* (1964, English 1967). The book reflected on war and post-war experiences. It also appeared in the midst of the student unrest in Germany and the United States.

Moltmann, a professor in Tübingen, looked like a businessman without any extraordinary features. But when he spoke, he was lively and eager to engage in debate. Moreover, he refused to be housed at the motel next to the campus because it was on the ground of the Gettysburg battlefield. "I cannot sleep on battlefields," he said, and then mentioned his time in the German army during the two final years of the war. So, we put him up in a downtown hotel, glad that he did not refuse to lecture on the battlefield!

I wanted to get his reaction to Karl Barth's critique that hope is not a "principle," as Bloch contended from an atheistic point of view, but trust in the "Trinitarian immanence" of God whose continual presence is assured in the "third time," the time beyond the last day. Moltmann told me that he was working on an eschatology that would go beyond Bloch and might be closer to Barth's.[4] I liked Moltmann's link of eschatology to ethics, viewed as liberation from the tyranny of oppression and exploitation. That is why Moltmann also became known as a proponent of "liberation theology." He made me reflect on what a Lutheran ethics might be. I leaned towards Barth who rejected the notion of an "independent ethics" which, in its most radical Lutheran version, assumes divine "orders of creation" (the state, marriage, and other orders).[5] Barth viewed moral action, like faith, grounded in divine revelation, rejecting any system of principles, rules, and regulations for Christian life in the world. Accordingly, Christians must discern what is "good" as the result of what needs to be done in specific situations as faithful disciples of Christ. Such ethics was taught by the young, German Lutheran theologian Dietrich Bonhoeffer (1906–1945) who defined the command, "Follow me," as the willingness to die (so stated in *The Cost of Discipleship*, 1937, English 1949). Both Bonhoeffer and Moltmann stressed the need for specific actions against worldly evils, be they tyranny, starvation, or other evils.

Soon after Moltmann's visit, I met one of his early colleagues at a guest lecture, **WOLFHART PANNENBERG** (1928–). Although both pursued a theology grounded in

---

4. Barth mailed his critique to Moltmann in a letter in 1964. See Barth, *Letters,* 174–76. Moltmann's continuing systematic work is in *The Crucified God,* (1972, English 1974) and *The Church and the Power of the Holy Spirit* (1975, English 1977).

5. The notion of unchanging institutions, such as marriage, government, and others, originated in the nineteenth century at the Lutheran University of Erlangen. Gottlieb Harless (1806–1879) is credited with its development.

eschatology, they were different as persons and thinkers. Pannenberg was very studious, slow in speaking, and quite immersed in a terminology of his own. But he had begun to become involved in an enduring controversy about his theology. So I had ascertained some biographical information and had perused his first two books, which had generated much critical dialogue, *Jesus: God and Man* (1964, English 1968) and *Revelation as History* (1967, English 1968). The first book argued that theology must find the "historical Jesus" and not separate him from the "Jesus of faith," as Protestant nineteenth-century theologians did. The second book, which includes essays by biblical scholars, contends that the revelation of God in Jesus is a "prolepsis" of the goal of history: just as the words at the beginning of a sentence anticipate the end of it, so does Christ's resurrection preview history and its end. Thus revelation creates the best understanding of the sequence of time. Pannenberg uses a variety of philosophical sources for his own hermeneutics, ranging from Plato to contemporary existentialist. This is the background of his attempt to combine Karl Barth, his teacher, and Hegel's philosophy of history. At this point, I got lost, even though I was quite taken by the attempt to "prove" the historicity of the divine revelation in Christ.

I invited some colleagues to my living room for a discussion with Pannenberg. Jenson liked him very much and claimed to know what he was about. But the guest seemed more immersed in his enduring curiosity for evermore ways of communicating his position than in teaching the group what he had found so far. His monotone speaking was accompanied by gestures with his hands. Moreover, his spouse, who behaved like a coach, often interrupted him and even tried to speak for him at times. I agreed with some of my colleagues that the encounter with Pannenberg was fascinating, but produced little, if any, perception of what he was about.

During his visit, Pannenberg had indicated his increasing involvement with science, especially its drive to explain the universe through cosmology. I read later that he had found a partner in the American cosmologist Frank Tipler who used Pannenberg's theology to advance his own "philosophy" in some publications, especially in a highly controversial book, *The Physics of Immortality* (1994); some called its content "pseudo science." Pannenberg created a small library of his own works culminating in a three-volume *Systematic Theology* (1988–93). He also spent some time in the United States as a guest professor in Chicago, Harvard, and other universities. I learned to appreciate his work as the Director of the Ecumenical Institute at the University of Munich. He became well known as a proponent for Christian unity through worship, linking his quest for Christianity as a source for universal truth with doxology as an expression of this "truth." Thus the Eucharist became for him the center of the ecumenical endeavor.

I had the chance of meeting the biggest "gun" among Roman Catholic theologians, **HANS KÜNG** (1928–) in Gettysburg where he lectured at the college during his stay as a visiting professor in Chicago in 1981. The office of the Campus Ministry at Gettysburg College seemed to be more able than the Seminary to afford such a world-renowned theologian. A native Swiss, Küng had first made a name for himself in the ecumenical movement through his doctoral dissertation in Paris on Karl Barth's doctrine of justification; it was published in English under the title, *Justification: The Doctrine of Karl Barth, and a Catholic Reflection* (1964).

Then he made a bad Catholic name for himself in the 1960s, during the Second Vatican Council, through his rejection of papal infallibility, published in English, *Infallibility? An Inquiry* (1970). The book caused Rome to strip him of the right to teach seminarians, but he retained all the privileges of a professor at the state university in Tübingen.

I cannot recall much of the Gettysburg lecture because it sounded as if it were done off the cuff; and it seemed to deal with the relationship of Christ and scientific inquiry, a topic Küng had begun to pursue with increasing attention.[6] I liked his work on Barth's doctrine of justification (as did Barth in a letter included in the book) because Küng showed very clearly that the differences between Protestants, like Barth, and Catholics who know Luther, are no longer divisive. In fact, the doctrine of papal infallibility, promulgated by the First Vatican Council in 1870, is more divisive (as Küng had contended).

In preparation for a fruitful discussion I read Küng's bestseller, *On Being a Christian* (1974). When I told him that I was one of the rare Lutherans in Austria and that I had attended a seminar of Barth in Basel in 1953 while he worked on his dissertation in Paris, he spent some time with me after the dinner to do some ecumenical shoptalk. He indicated that he was more interested in the unity of humankind than in Christian unity, which seemed to be a lofty goal. Küng exhibited an unassuming demeanor, looking like a mountain climber rather than an academician. He loved questions from the students and ended our conversation with a firm handshake. I continue to read him and about

---

6. His mature reflections are offered in his recent book, *The Beginning of All Things: Science and Religion* (2007).

him. He embodies for me an evangelical-Catholic stance with a clear vision of the power of the gospel in an increasingly complex world. Encountering him suggests to me that Christian work for global justice may be a better option than trying to persuade Rome to view its tradition as equal with other traditions and join the cause for Christian unity.[7]

During a year's sabbatical in Heidelberg, Germany, I encountered **HEINRICH BORNKAMM** (1901–1977), the "dean" of German Luther research. I had just completed the translation of his seminal book *Luther and the Old Testament* (1969, German 1948), and my Müntzer book had been published a year earlier. So I could stand on a small ground of scholarly achievement—an important condition for meeting Bornkamm. He was a very polite and formal scholar known for his careful defense of Luther. Students said that scheduled conferences with him seemed to be "audiences" rather than appointments. Since I was no longer a student but a seminary professor who had made the grade with a successful book in Reformation studies, Bornkamm's specialty, I was invited for afternoon tea at his home. When I arrived, he and his spouse were very gracious hosts. I brought greetings from my "doctor father" Bainton who knew Bornkamm well. Then we talked about my work as a translator and about the "Radical Reformation." Bornkamm told me that one of his former students, now an instructor, taught a seminar on the "Anabaptists" and that I should speak about the American research on the subject. When I did a few weeks later, I

---

7. In the 1990s Küng organized a Foundation for a Global Ethic (*Weltethos*), sketched in his book *A Global Ethic for Politics and Economics* (1997). It is supported by the Parliament of World Religions (1993) and the United Nations Dialogue Among Civilizations, with Küng as one of nineteen "eminent persons."

discovered that the seminar had not dealt with American contributions to research in the "Radical Reformation" even though most of the seminar members handled English quite well. So I filled the entire blackboard with a bibliography and conducted a very animated discussion, continued with beer in one of the historic student hangouts.

Bornkamm invited me to attend an evening colloquy with several remaining doctoral students at his home and to present a paper of my choice for discussion. I decided to do the paper on a topic that had been treated half a century earlier by the famous Luther scholar Karl Holl, the "father" of Luther research at the beginning of the twentieth century, well respected by Bornkamm. The topic was presented in German, titled "Luther and the 'Swarmers': Rejected *Anfechtung* [*Schwärmer*, Luther's nickname for his enemies whom he viewed as a swarm of wild bees]." The paper was later published in Germany.[8] I summarized new research done by Bainton at Yale, Williams at Harvard, and by others, contending that the wholesale rejection of the Schwärmer by Luther and Holl was unfair and that both would have learned to cherish the views of quite a few radicals if they had studied them. After all, Mennonites and other "Anabaptists" survived as pacifists and defenders of causes that served humanity better than did some Catholic and mainline Protestant groups. The paper caused a lively discussion, with Bornkamm defending Luther as a "man of his time" who should not be judged on the basis of modern

---

8. Gritsch, "Luther and the Radicals: Rejected *Anfechtung*," 105–21. Luther scholars try not to translate the word *Anfechtung*. It is used by Luther for "temptation" (*tentatio* in Latin). But its contextual meaning varies. It became Luther's favorite expression to describe the attacks of Satan and/or struggle with God.

assumptions. When I referred to Luther's well-known treatises against the Jews, calling for their persecution later enacted by Nazi Germany, using Luther's writings, Bornkamm almost lost his cool and called Luther's so-called anti-Semitism an "appendix" to his work, generated by disease and old age. The "Bornkamm Luther" just could not do any wrong. Today, hardly any serious Luther scholar holds such a view. But my aggressive paper did not end my relationship with Bornkamm during my Heidelberg year. He was a true scholar and gentleman. Unfortunately, he died before completing a massive Luther biography.

My other, totally different, encounter in Heidelberg was with the icon of patristic studies (the "church fathers" of the first centuries) **HANS VON CAMPENHAUSEN** (1903–1989). He was not only an outstanding church historian but also "stood out" in any assembly, certainly in the Heidelberg theological faculty, as a peculiar, indeed idiosyncratic personality. Born into a family of German nobles in Russia, he looked like an Orthodox priest who had given up his call: bearded, bespectacled, smoking big cigars, and living without a telephone. One of his American doctoral students told me that Campenhausen taught a seminar on "The Wit of Tertullian" (Latin church father at the end of the second century, known for his satirical polemics). It was the only event with loud laughter in the somber halls of Heidelberg University! Campenhausen also collected early Christian jokes and published four hundred of them under the title, *Fun and Jokes among Theologians: Almost 400* (*Theologenspiess-und Spass: kaum 400*, 1973).

I went to his evening class on the Origins of the Christian Bible (published in English as *The Formation of the Christian Bible*, 1968). When I introduced myself to him after the class, he said, "Oh, you don't need this course. It is for beginners." I told him that his book on the origins of the ordained ministry and its authority in the early church had been essential in shaping my view of ecclesiastical authority (*Ecclesiastical Authority and Spiritual Power in the Church of the First Centuries*, 1953, English 1969). When I returned from Heidelberg, I organized a seminar on the topic; it became a regular feature of my teaching. I met him one more time in a café for an extended discussion (smoking one of his big cigars). His knowledge of early church history was phenomenal, exemplified in the publication of three volumes with the biographies of all known Greek and Latin church fathers. I was tempted, but did not dare to ask him or Bornkamm, whether a story about his contribution to a faculty celebration of Bornkamm's birthday was true: allegedly, Campenhausen appeared with a long role of toilet paper inscribed with various comments about Bornkamm's virtues and achievements. Having encountered this peculiar Heidelberg icon, I have no difficulties believing that the incident happened!

My friend at Yale, Jim Holloway, introduced me to the most unusual, indeed idiosyncratic, American theologian, political churchman, musician, and novelist, **WILL CAMPBELL** (1924–). Only in America could the likes of him be found! I met him first in an elegant bar in New York City during the final phases of the widespread protests against racism and the war in Vietnam. When the bartender asked him, "What would you like, Sir?" Campbell, who was dressed in a formal dark suit and wore a furry trappers' cap with a tail in the back, responded, "A double Kentucky Sour Mash [bourbon] with a shot of branch water." My friend Jim translated the order when the bartender showed a puzzled face. "Just give him a bourbon with water."

This Baptist preacher from Mississippi—a Yale graduate, a guitar-playing country singer, a writer, and a prophet condemning violence, especially the death penalty, marching with Martin Luther King—shared my interest in the sixteenth-century radical reformers as victims of injustice. I read his book *The Glad River* (1982), a novel depicting Dutch "Anabaptists," also known as "water-minded" (*Doopsgesinde*), twentieth-century people, represented by three young men who announce their baptism in the morning paper: a complete immersion in an electrically heated tub. Campbell's way of writing had become best known in memoirs and novels, such as *Brother to a Dragon Fly* (1977) and *Up to the Steeples in Politics* (with James Holloway in 1980). He called one night and told me that the story of Baptists in *The Glad River* was linked to the fate of a woman and two men who lived four hundred years earlier. Some of their descendants appeared in the genealogy of his Southern family. He had written a novella about them, titled, *Cecilia's Sin*. Would I write "A Historical Introduction"? I said, "Of course." The novella appeared in 1983.

Will and I kept in touch, meeting at Berea College where his friend Jim Holloway taught and edited the *Journal of the Committee of Southern Churchmen, Katallagete* (Be Reconciled). I never forget a sermon on the evil of the death penalty, delivered at Gettysburg College; the vivid eyewitness description of an execution caused several listeners to pass out. A man of few seasons!

Early in my career I had met **GÜNTHER GASSMANN** (1931–), Director of the Faith and Order Commission of the World Council of Churches (WCC). During a break at an ecumenical conference I heard jazz music from a piano and, tracing it, encountered the German Lutheran guest lecturer from Geneva. Others joined me to enjoy this unexpected entertainment. When it ended with haunting sounds of the blues, I made a beeline to the piano and asked, "How come? A German theologian playing like a pianist in a New Orleans band?" When we talked one on one, he told me that during the first years after the war he added jazz music to his classical repertoire and, to make money, he created a band with fellow students in Heidelberg, playing primarily for Americans who had set up military headquarters in the town and hired bands for their socials.

Gassmann embodied global ecumenism, being the theological voice of The World Council of Churches at its meetings dealing with doctrine ("Faith and Order"); the other arm of the organization was "Life and Work." I invited him to Gettysburg and Washington DC, where ecumenical dialogue was incorporated into the curriculum of theological schools through a consortium (Lutheran, Roman Catholic, Anglican, and Methodist). Gassmann was a lively lecturer, using his own experiences as illustrations of the ecumenism that flowered after Vatican II that ended its work in 1965. He spoke with his back bent, as if he were focusing on piano keys, looking up to this audience, and using his arms to make a point.

As Distinguished Guest Professor at the seminary, he taught courses on ecumenism and on the Lutheran Confessions; he co-authored the *Fortress Introduction to the Lutheran Confessions* (with Scott Hendrix in 1999) and in cooperation with others he published a *Historical Dictionary of Lutheranism* (2002). We became good friends. He demonstrated to me that solid, serious ecumenical work overcomes the always threatening "winter of discontent."

The whetstone of my mind, as it were, was **JOHN LOOSE** (1927–1987) on the faculty of religion at Gettysburg College. I met him shortly after my arrival in Gettysburg when I watched a soccer match in the small college stadium. The coach, a short, stocky man, directed the home team with various hand motions and some quiet talk, moving on the sidelines, wearing sunglasses, and smoking a cigarillo. When I inquired about him, a student told me, "Oh, that is Professor Loose who became the most successful coach without ever touching a ball. He is also quite a teacher. We put a sign on his office door, reading in bold letters "Hang Loose.""

As soon as the game was over, with an overwhelming victory of the home team, I introduced myself to the coach, referring to my experience with soccer as soon as I could kick a ball (I ended up playing left wing on my school team). Loose grinned and said, "Well, I have heard that you are on the seminary faculty as an imported player." The remark disclosed John's typical mixture of scholarly detective work and satirical communication. We went to my home, had a drink, and talked until about midnight, getting to know each other. John had graduated from the Gettysburg Seminary, then did graduate studies in the field of "Religion and Literature" at the University of Chicago, focusing on the eminent, left-wing British poet W. H. Auden (1907–1973) who had received the Pulitzer Prize for *The Age of Anxiety* (1947). He was still working on his dissertation when we met. John's biography was fascinating: raised a Mennonite,[9]

---

9. Named after Menno Simons, a sixteenth-century "Anabaptist" pacifist leader from Frisia on the Dutch coast. Guided by a vision of a new moral life, based on being in "a new creation" (2 Cor 5:17), he led his followers to a life separated from the evils of the world dominated by

he deserted his family, joined the marines, advanced to the rank of drill sergeant; left the army and worked in a steel mill; got a pilot's license to make money as a crop duster; married and had seven children; known as a crack teacher and sharp debater; a soccer coach who, studying theories of the game, taught his team winning combinations based on a hard discipline of mind and body. When I met him, the team had won several conference championships. "Why get into soccer?" I asked. "It's like chess," John said. "The moves are more interesting than winning, and the game has made players excellent students."

During the many years at Gettysburg, John and I hardly agreed on anything in our long discussions of theological and philosophical issues. He always challenged what I tried to assert, even my cherished notion of "hope" for a future after death. "What is the real evidence for hope?" John asked about "insurance." "Faith," I said. "As it is written, 'faith is the assurance of things hoped for, the conviction of things not seen'" (Heb 11:1). John retorted, "Is 'faith' an 'assurance' like that made by an insurance company?"—and another endless discussion began. Perhaps because of his Mennonite roots, John accepted as "real" only what could be done, not just what is said or thought. When he discovered that the maintenance crew at the college was badly underpaid, compared to similar work outside the college, he debated the matter in a faculty meeting with such parliamentary skill and convincing evidence that the administration grudgingly consented "to do justice" (as John put it). He played a similar role in the

---

violence. Mennonites summarized their teachings in "The Schleitheim Articles," 1527, English text in John C. Wenger, "The Schleitheim Confession of Faith," *The Mennonite Quarterly Review* 19 (1945) 243–54.

movements for racial justice and against the Vietnam War in the 1960s. John cradled my knowledge of American literature, novels, poetry, and essays. His untimely death deprived me of the sharpening of my mind.

PART FOUR

Special Engagements

"Publish or Parish"

9

International Congress for Luther Research

(1964–2002)

As I worked my way from the most radical of the "radical reformers" of the sixteenth century, Thomas Müntzer, to the most conservative mainline reformer, Martin Luther, the timing was right when I was invited by Dantine to join the assembly of about two hundred Luther scholars who met every four or five years in August to discuss and to show off their work. While in Europe there is the fear of "publish or perish," in the United States ordained theologians like myself hear of the threat "publish or parish." I had published some papers on the "Radical Reformation" and on Luther, knowing that the Congress expected publications as a foundation for the expected scholarly dialogue. So I, like others, wrote a book on the occasion of the five hundred anniversary of his birth in 1983, *Martin—God's Court Jester: Luther in Retrospect*. The Congress had been established in 1956, and Dantine arranged my attendance at the third meeting in 1966 in Järvenpää, near Helsinki, Finland, on the theme "The Church, Mysticism, Sanctification, and the Natural." German and English were the used languages. Dantine was not a Luther scholar in a narrow sense, but he stayed involved with a Luther paper here and there. Besides, there were no clear rules about membership, and the ad hoc committees arranged the conferences. German, Scandinavian, and American scholars constituted a majority at the Congress, with a sprinkling of British, French, and Asian scholars (Japan, South Korea, and China).

I learned most from the Scandinavians and the Germans, including Roman Catholics who appeared for the first time in 1966 in the spirit of reforms proposed by the Second Vatican Council (1959–65). I had read two publications by the president of the Third Congress, **LENNART PINOMAA** (1901–1996): *Temptation as the Background of the Gospel in Luther's Theology* (*Anfechtung als Hintergrund des Evangeliums in der Theologie Luthers*, 1943) and *Faith Victorious: An Introduction to Luther's Theology* (1963). He was a tall, slender Finn who invited participants to join him in the Finnish ritual of the sauna experience in the Lutheran church camp where the conference took place, a deserted wooded area outside the small town of Järvenpää, near the lonely tomb of the composer Johan Sibelius (1855–1951). There was a primitive building with sweat baths where one birched oneself before diving, or walking, into a very cold lake. The health ritual concluded in a room with fellowship around a big fireplace stacked with liquor, beer, food, and cigars. Dantine, others, and I used to similar adventures during and after the war, joined Pinomaa in a procession to the baths. He entered and stayed in them in the nude; a small group, myself included, did likewise. But some of the Lutheran "big guns" huddled together, trying to decide what to do. This was the only gathering of scholars that included such an esoteric, indeed embarrassing feature. But while the Lutherans hesitated, the Catholic group, consisting of almost only monks, stripped and followed Pinomaa into the sauna.

During the weeklong proceedings I had a chance to talk to Pinomaa about Luther's experience of *Anfechtung*. My initial reading of Luther stressed the psychological aspect of his experience. Pinomaa showed that it was deeply anchored in Luther's view of the Word of God as "law" (mandates for living) and "gospel" (eschatological promise of a sinless future). *Anfechtung* was a bridge between the two, plowing up a guilty conscience and planting faith as a divine gift enabling survival, "faith victorious." Finnish culture, with its very special language (related only to Hungarian) and artistic expression (the music of Sibelius), seemed to be better tuned to the young Luther than other cultures. Be that as it may, Pinomaa opened up a new door to my nascent Luther research.

GUSTAF WINGREN (1910–2000) was the Swedish Luther scholar who moved my interest to Luther's ethics in two popular books, *Luther on Vocation* (1942 and other editions) and *Creation and Law* (1961). My week in Finland made it possible for me to discuss his differences with Karl Barth on "vocation:" Barth viewed Christian vocation as life under the gospel without any guidance by divine "law." Wingren adopted Luther's description of vocation as life in two divine realms ("kingdoms"), the realms of sin (revealed by the law) and the realm of faith in Christ (granted by the gospel). I sided with Luther and Wingren, even though I still was attracted to Barth's single-minded Christ-centered theology.

When I met Wingren again at another Congress, he criticized the church (especially in Sweden) for having become lax in Christian catechesis as the instrument for creating and preserving "work" (vocation) as a service of love of neighbor rather than just a "job" for maintaining a comfortable life. His target was the political system in Sweden where everything had become "socialized" from cradle to grave; the "state church" was an integral part of the system maintained by taxes. He also had changed his appearance as a professor at Lund: he wore informal clothes, married a radical Socialist after a widely discussed divorce, and he refused to lecture on anything else but "marriage" as the only trustworthy "vocation." Former students, especially from the United States, were perplexed, indeed shocked, when they met their revered teacher, accompanied by his second wife (young, chain-smoking, with a dress fashionable in the 1920s, and wearing a French barrette), talking to his first wife (who looked like a matron at home in Swedish high society). Wingren seemed to be his good old self. When I talked to him about Barth, he affirmed the obvious disagreement without mentioning marriage as the ideal vocation. Given Wingren's personal situation, I let the matter rest.

I also met **REGIN PRENTER** (1907–1990), the Danish systematic theologian who had written a seminal book on Luther and the "radical reformers" focusing on the Holy Spirit, *Spiritus Creator* (1944, English 1946). It was a major source for my doctoral dissertation which investigated the "authority of the inner word," the claim to possess the Holy Spirit as the authority that is higher than the "outer word" of the Bible. The "Spiritualists," as George Williams at Harvard dubbed them, constituted an influential group of the "Radical Reformation," Thomas Müntzer being the first among them. Prenter knew my book about him; so we shared a common interest. I told him that his work was my bridge to move from the opponents of Luther in his own camp to him, the subject of my enduring interest. Prenter had clearly elaborated Luther's view of the Holy Spirit as an integral part of the Trinity over against the view of the sixteenth-century Spiritualists who extracted the "third person" as the dominant one. That is why second-generation Spiritualists became anti-Trinitarians, or Unitarians. I told Prenter that his work had confirmed my theological suspicion that Luther's designation of Müntzer and other "radicals" as *Schwärmer* and heretics was quite appropriate albeit without a call to kill them.

I enjoyed meeting the pleasant professor from Aarhus University. I saw him again at other Congresses, together with other Danes, some of whom were his students. Among them was **LEIF GRANE** (1928–2000) from the University of Copenhagen who would become a close friend. He and Dantine were friends, sharing critical views of Lutheranism and the church in general. Regarding Luther research, Grane worked intensively with texts from the younger Luther, trying to show how he became a reformer within Catholicism. I was quite taken by his minute analysis of Luther's writings, beginning in 1515, two years before he wrote his famous *Ninety-Five Theses,* and ending one year later, in 1518, with his critical farewell to the Catholic medieval scholastic theology, *The Way Theology Should be Done: Luther's Combat for the Renewal of Theology, 1515–1518* (*Modus Loquendi Theologicus: Luthers Kampf um die Erneuerung der Theologie, 1515–1518,* 1975).

Dissatisfied with the discussions at the Congress, Grane invited Dantine, a few other scholars, and me for a "minicongress," as it were, at his home in Copenhagen. Treated with excellent Danish food and drink (the famous brandy *aquavit,* chased with beer), I learned much from Grane and his guests. He proposed that at the Congress over which he was to preside, in 1977 in Lund, Sweden, there should be debate between Lutherans and Catholics, modeled after the famous "Leipzig Debate" between Luther and John Eck in 1519. He successfully persuaded the planning committee to schedule a debate on the thesis, "Luther's Success and Failure as a Reformer of the Church." A planning committee, consisting of Lutherans and Catholics, chose the two debaters, Albert Brandenburg from the Roman Catholic Academy in Paderborn, Germany, and I. Since Bandenburg was not fluent in English, the debate was conducted in German. Since Grane told me to put some life into the debate (Brandenburg was known to be pedantic), I titled my explication of the topic with a parody of Luther's famous *Ninety-Five Theses* of 1517: "Nine and One Half Theses. Presented out of love, a zeal for Lutheranism as a reform movement within the church catholic, and by mandate of the Continuation Committee for the Fifth International Congress for Luther Research, meeting August 14 to 20 1977 in Lund, Sweden."[1] My half thesis stated that Luther *failed* to do his work in such a way as to produce a consensus among Luther scholars; but he *succeeded* in creating the Luther Congress that might finally recognize him as a legitimate "father of the church." No formal decision was made, in contrast to the debate in 1519, regarding a winner and looser. But there was an informal "party" by Lutherans and Catholics declaring that I had won it. Grane was satisfied.

We stayed in touch with each other until his untimely death. He was a man who might have been a court jester

---

1. Text of both presentations in Grane and Lohse, *Luther und die Theologie der Gegenwart*, 97–111. Also in Gritsch, *The Boy*, 317–25.

at a royal court, telling unwelcome truths to the high and mighty who only tolerated truth in the disguise of wit. I admire his work, not only in Luther research, but also in Lutheranism, exemplified by his widely used commentary on the Augsburg Confession of 1530.

I encountered a new, very creative, and controversial interpretation of Luther by the Finnish Luther scholar **TUOMO MANNERMAA** (1937–). When the Lutheran Church in Finland initiated a dialogue with the small Finnish Orthodox Church, he used his new approach to Luther as a link between the two communions. In addition, he persuaded a number of doctoral students to join him in his research, resulting in a new "school" of Luther studies. I had begun reading his papers on Luther's view of "justification." He contended that, "justification" as the "work "of Christ is not only declared as a judgment, promising to be free of sin after the resurrection, but is also the presence of Christ in the believer. The popular dogmatic Lutheran view of a "forensic justification" (similar to a verdict in a court or forum) misses its full power, already known by Luther, namely, a divinizing (*theosis* in Greek) of the believing person. But the introduction of the Greek designation for this process immediately caused Lutheran opposition because Greek Orthodox theology uses the term to define a mystical-sacramental "deification" evident already in the earthly life of believers. The debate with the Finnish school continues; Mannermaa has summarized the results of his work in the book *Christ Present in Faith: Luther's View of Justification* (2005).

Since I had become aware of the doxological-liturgical aspect of justification in the classic Lutheran definition of the gospel as "word and sacrament," I wondered about

Christ's "real" presence in the Eucharist and in the believer. Mannermaa made it very clear that he did not teach a Greek Orthodox "theosis."

A long conversation with him convinced me of that, but also attracted me to his hermeneutical decision to distinguish no longer between the "person" and "work" of Christ. German neo-Kantian philosophers (disciples of Immanuel Kant, 1724–1804) had defined "being" in terms of relationships, disclosed in the intricate system of the universe. Mannermaa contended that what a person is and does define human "being." Accordingly, Luther research, especially in Germany, is shortsighted when it is based on a neo-Kantian hermeneutics. I also found in the creedal description of the relationship between Christ, the Son of God, and the Holy Spirit ("who also proceeds from the Father and the Son"—Nicene Creed) a similar view. When a special Congress session was devoted to a discussion of Manneraa's position, German Luther scholars rejected it; I was part of a small minority that defended him because I had read about Christ's presence in the believer in a number of Luther's sermons, especially those preached in the Christmas season. Luther scholars tend to neglect the sermons.

Among the German Luther scholars, I met **BERNHARD LOHSE** (1928–1997) who has crowned his rich meticulous research in a masterful summary of Luther's theology, *Martin Luther's Theology: Its Historical and Systematic Development* (German 1997, English 1999). He was a good friend of Leif Grane who introduced me to him. While Grane was a "happy Dane," witty and controversial, Lohse was a dignified, quiet academician who, however, would let his hair down in a stag party with good food and drinks. He was fluent in Oxford English so that I was able to invite him to lectures at Gettysburg, as one institution among others that also invited him, thus sharing expenses.

My encounter with Lohse, however, yielded some "negative learning" because of his treatment of "Luther's attitude to the Jews," a hot topic in the United States highlighted by the quincentenary of Luther's birth in 1983. In his lengthy summary of Luther's theology, he devoted six pages to the topic in an "excursus" at the end of the book (with 393 pages). Moreover, he totally ignored the intensive treatment of the topic in the United Stares. I had summarized the literature with an analysis of Luther's rejection of the Jews in my Luther book. After a long discussion, Lohse granted that the topic needed more attention. But he disagreed with others and me that Luther's stance was the result of a serious fault in his theological reflections.[2] I discovered that most of the German Luther scholars blocked any attempt to devote a Congress session to this neuralgic topic—a lesson in the relationship between research and politics.

The "big gun" at the Congresses was **GERHARD EBELING** (1912–2001), although he attended only several times. He was renowned as a Luther scholar through three volumes of *Luther Studies (Lutherstudien*, 1971–89), as the creator of a "new hermeneutics" through four volumes of *Word and Faith* (1960–95), and as the author of a three-volume *Dogmatics of the Christian Faith* (*Dogmatik des christ-*

---

2. Luther agreed with the medieval Christian "theology of supersession" which taught that God shifted his love for Jews to the Christians because Jews refused to convert, and Luther used this assumed divine shift to call for a Christian rejection of the Jews, implemented in a policy of persecution resembling that of the Hitler regime in Germany. See chapter 7, "The Gospel and Israel," in my book *Martin—God's Court Jester*.

lichen Glaubens, 1979). Moreover, in the 1930s he had been a seminarian in Dietrich Bonhoeffer's secret Finkenwald Seminary, and he served as an underground pastor of the German "Confessing Church" during World War II, escaping from persecution to Switzerland where he taught at Zurich. Even Grane controlled his bubbling conversation in the presence of Ebeling. I never dared to approach him. But he surprised me when he moved to my seat during the meeting of the Congress in Lund in 1977 and congratulated me for my disputation! Just a few words and a handshake from a man who spoke softly, but carried a big stick in academia; but he seemed to be humble and genuine in his appreciation of the young, American debater. I remember his face: clean-shaven with glasses, tired-looking eyes with dark rings under them, and lips that hardly moved when he spoke one on one (yet with a strong voice in public).

In an imagined encounter, I would have asked him why, as a Lutheran, he preferred to speak of "word and faith" rather than of "word and sacrament" and why he did not have a chapter on sacraments in his popular *Introduction to Luther's Thought* (1971). After all, Luther spent much of his time defending the presence of Christ in the Eucharist against *Schwärmer* who denied it. But I did not dare to launch an offensive against Ebeling in a brief dialogue since he was not known to correct himself even after extensive feuds. He stuck to his "new hermeneutics," developed in close cooperation with the existentialist New Testament scholar Rudolf Bultmann who viewed the de-mythologized "word" about Christ as "proof" of his historical reality in the person of Jesus of Nazareth. That is why "word" and "faith" are the foundations of Christianity.³ I sometimes wonder in a dream whether a heavenly faculty of theology would continue to debate the "new hermeneutics" of Bultmann and Ebeling or request a clarification by the Trinity!

Ebeling's protege was the Reformed Dutch scholar **HEIKO OBERMAN** (1930–2001). I met him first in Harvard while I taught at Wellesley College. Williams had invited him, a German colleague, and me for dinner and discussion of our experiences in Europe. Oberman was a lively participant, disclosing his ambition to forge a new approach to Reformation and Luther studies. He offered his new insights in a book that impressed Ebeling, *The Harvest of Medieval Theology* (1963). It contended that there was continuity rather than a break between Luther and late medieval theology. Soon thereafter Ebeling successfully lobbied for Oberman's call to Tübingen, Germany, as the Director of the Institute for Late Medieval and Reformation Studies. There he organized his research like a general on the battlefield, using doctoral students and a Dutch publisher.

From there, he traveled widely as a lecturer. One of his cherished topics was "anti-Semitism," with particular attention to Luther's polemics against the Jews.

---

3. Rudolf Bultmann (1884–1976) began a long inconclusive debate in 1941 with a proposal to "de-mythologize" the New Testament by rejecting its ancient view of a universe in which the earth was flat. That proposal renewed the old debate about the "Jesus of history" and the "Christ of faith." Bultmann and Ebeling tried to use existentialist philosophy to define "historicity" as an indissoluble fusion of fact and meaning, expressed in "word" and "faith." Bultmann's unsuccessful attempts to convert his opponents are collected in four volumes of essays published between 1933 and 1960. English summary of proposals in Bultmann, *Kerygma and Myth* (1961).

Unlike Lohse, who relegated them to a sideline of his Luther studies, Oberman put them into the center of his Luther research. During his visit to Gettysburg, he told me, after an emotional presentation of Luther's significance for later generations, that one should not do a biography of Luther unless one had studied the history of Christian anti-Semitism. When asked why, he mentioned his memory as a boy in Holland, seeing Jews transported to the infamous German death camps. I surmised that this might also have been a reason why he wanted to outdo German scholars. Be that as it may, he first published *The Roots of Anti-Semitism* a year before the celebration of Luther's five-hundredth birthday in 1983. Then he offered his interpretation of Luther, *Man between God and the Devil* (German 1987, English 1989). I was the first to review it.[4] It was a critical review, calling the book "not a biography, but an apologia for a revisionist thesis about Luther and the Reformation." Oberman tried to show that Luther, like an Old Testament prophet, proclaimed "the reformation to come," after the last day. Thus he was neither medieval nor modern, but one who presented anew the original Christian message of Christ's victory over sin, death, and evil (the devil).

I expected to experience the sting of his polemics against those who differed with him. But there was silence, even after we saw each other several times at various occasions. But I remember him as a passionate scholar who was moved by simple, indeed naive, experiences like his childhood experiences of anti-Semitism, as well as by a drive to find an ever-new approach to research. I vividly recall how he fell on his knees at the end of a lecture on anti-Semitism,

---

4. See *Church History* 60 (1991), 383–85.

then rose to his full, impressive height and said, with his heavy Dutch accent: "Enough for now. I must stop and fly to Australia." During his final career stop at the University of Arizona, he organized an American version of his Tübingen Institute and made it very popular through a "Town and Gown" lecture series, raising millions of dollars to assure its longevity. I learned from him what to do and what not do in the complex field of Reformation and Luther studies.

MARTIN BRECHT (1932–) impressed me with his three-volume biography of Luther, *Martin Luther* (German 1981–87, English 1990–93). I read it during a roundtrip train journey from Hamburg to Oslo and talked with him at some of the Congresses. Teaching at Münster (the city that rhymes with "Müntzer," my first research subject), he was a lively historian who analyzed every aspect of Luther's life and thought—an amazing achievement. I had asked Bainton how he wrote his one-volume biography of Luther, and he showed me a large folder that contained eight versions of *Here I Stand*, many manuscript pages pasted together to improve the flow of the story. Brecht told me that he, like most German professors, had graduate students as assistants who were to help him in everything except in writing. When the translation was arranged, he asked me to spot-check various parts since he knew me as an editor and translator of two volumes of the American edition of selected works of Luther.[5] I did the checking, told him that I knew the translator, and that the massive work would be in good American hands.

Brecht was a short, stocky man who reminded me of my *Gymnnasium* mathematics teacher who also was the coach

---

5. Vols. 39 and 41 of *Luther's Works*.

of the school's soccer team. Like the coach, he got quickly excited, indeed annoyed, when things became confused, often by a violation of rules; but afterwards he apologized for having lost his cool. I recall Brecht's brief, angry comments when someone used a plenary session of the Congress for a long, off-the-cuff diatribe. Brecht rose from his seat and angrily told the violator of the program that he was out of order. "If we end up like this, I am going to pack my bags and go home." Then he left. The program committee invited Brecht and some colleagues who knew him well to attend a meeting to deal with the incident. In the morning, Brecht was at the lectern before another plenary session. "Dear Colleagues," he said quietly, "please, accept my apology for what I did yesterday. As you can see, I decided to stay." There was polite applause, and the Congress was back on track. I, for one, imagined that Luther would have applauded Brecht for stopping a wiseacre.

OSWALD BAYER (1939–), the German theologian from Tübingen, taught me why and how Luther is much needed in the contemporary world. I had met Bayer in Gettysburg when he did a presentation of his favorite philosopher, Johann Georg Hamann (1730–1788), who was one of the architects of the movement of romanticism as an alternative to the European Enlightenment. Bayer found in Hamann a sense of beauty, expressed in poetic literature and worship, as well as a positive experience of change through an inner struggle, indeed a conversion. Hamann compared it to the visit of the "wise men" who were "overwhelmed with joy" when they saw the baby Jesus (Matt 2:10). He became known as the "Magus of the North."

Bayer was shaped in his thinking and speaking by Hamann, looking like a kind schoolteacher who wanted to persuade students to use their minds beyond traditional logic and to develop deeper insights, indeed even a sensitivity for mystery and beauty. He used Hamann's insights in his second, inaugural dissertation of 1970 (*Habilitation*) to elaborate Luther's inner struggle as the enduring encounter of the believer with God grounded in the divine "promise" (*promissio*) of salvation. The dissertation was published in 1989, titled, *Promissio: The History of Luther's Theological Break-Through* (*Geschichte der reformatorischen Wendung in Luthers Theologie*). He told me about his work on another book, showing how Luther's insights are significant in the contemporary world (*Luther's Theology: A Contemporary Interpretation*, German 1994, English 2007).

I shared with Bayer my dissatisfaction with the Luther depicted by Ebeling and his "school" who viewed the gospel "promise" as a "word event" (*Wortgeschehen*), neglecting its equally significant power as a "sacramental event" (*Sakramentsgeschehen*). In this sense, the gospel is proclaimed *and* celebrated. This was Bayer's impressive way in which Luther's theology "becomes contemporary" (is *vergegenwärtigt*).

American Lutheran church historian **JAROSLAV PELIKAN** (1923–2006) pioneered the ecumenical approach to Luther. Just before my first attendance at the Congress in Finland in 1964, I had read Pelikan's much-discussed book *Obedient Rebels: Catholic Substance and Protestant Principle in Luther's Reformation* (1962). As a former member of the tiny Lutheran church in my native "Catholic Austria" (6 percent Lutherans), I had begun to search for an alternative to the popular interpretation of Luther as a hostile protester and founder of a schismatic church. Pelikan provided such an alternative by using Paul Tillich's well-known dialectic of "substance" and "principle." "Substance," according to Pelikan's Luther, is "the body of tradition" (liturgy, dogma, churchmanship) represented in the Roman Catholic Church; and "principle" is the gospel-criticism of this tradition. Luther, therefore, does not want to abolish Catholicism but to reconstruct it as a more faithful witness to the gospel in the Bible.

When I met Pelikan in Finland he had continued his meteoric rise as the foremost American historian of the Christian tradition and, in his final years, as a historian of non-Christian doctrines. He quickly let it be known, almost in any conversation or public lecture, that he was a descendant of the Czech Hussites, also known as the Bohemian or Moravian Brethren represented in America by the Lutheran Slovak Synod.[6] Pelikan was the son of a Lutheran pastor in the synod and a grandson of a Hussite bishop in Bohemia. In 1998, Pelikan joined the Orthodox Church in the United States.

Pelikan looked like a longshoreman who had become a professor: a robust man, clean-shaven, wearing gasses, and dressed in a business suit. His boisterous laugh drew people to him in social gatherings, especially when American martinis were served. He quickly organized transportation by taxis to and from the rare Finnish drinking places during the Congress. I could easily connect with him as Bainton's

---

6. John Hus (c. 1369–1415) opposed the papacy and was martyred for his views. His disciples, the "Hussites," first responded with military force, then went underground, and finally emerged as pacifist "Bohemian Brethren" (in a part of Czechoslovakia). Supported by the Lutheran "Pietist" Nicholas von Zinzendorf, they established an enduring community of farmers and craftsmen in 1727 in Saxony called "Herrnhut" ("the watch of the Lord"). They adhered to the Lutheran Augsburg Confession. See Gritsch, *A History of Lutheranism*, 152–53.

student at Yale where Pelikan had begun to teach in 1962; my work on Müntzer linked me with the Hussites because this radical reformer spent some time in Prague, trying to lead a new Hussite reform movement as an alternative to Luther's.

Pelikan chaired the Congress in St. Louis in 1971 in America, and came to Gettysburg to do a lecture on "Luther Comes to America."[7] He drove a Porsche sports car and almost exhausted my supply of martinis! Years later, after my retirement, we met again in Baltimore where he lectured at the Catholic Seminary on the history of Christian doctrine "in slow motion" (singling out some events for special consideration). He grew a beard while laboring on his five volumes of the history of the Christian tradition. His friends claimed that he wanted to be the American impersonation of the great German historian of doctrine, Adolf von Harnack (1851–1930). I did not dare to ask him about it. I owe him a great debt of gratitude for turning my attention to Lutheranism as a reform movement within the Catholic Church—a point of view my colleague Robert Jenson and I advocated in our exposition of the sixteenth-century Lutheran Confessions, *Lutheranism* (1976).

I also learned much from the Lutheran American expert on Humanism and Renaissance, **LEWIS SPITZ** (1922–1999), who taught at Stanford University in California. In the early 1960s, I read some of his essays on Luther's link to Humanism; they were collected in *Luther and German Humanism* (1996) and incorporated into the two-volume study *The Renaissance and Reformation Movements* (1980). Spitz exposed the issue of the relationship between faith

---

7. Lecture available in Gritsch, *Encounters with Luther*, 1:58–66.

and reason in the famous debate between Luther and the Humanist Erasmus of Rotterdam: can one make a rational decision for or against conversion to Christ (as Erasmus contended), or is the human will so weakened by sin that it can only be moved to conversion by faith alone, granted by the Holy Spirit (as Luther argued)? Spitz tried to find some common ground between Luther and the Humanists who, above all, stressed a "return to original sources" (*ad fontes*)—disclosed in Luther's claim that the Bible has the highest authority in the church as the mediator of the Word of God. Spitz, like others and myself, had found significant hermeneutical insights in the work of Wilhelm Dilthey (1833–1911).[8] If one views human freedom in terms of time rather than in terms of a timeless Aristotelian logic, it is only "relatively," not "absolutely," free. Such a view leaves more space for some accommodations between "faith" and "reason" since they are bound by the limitations of time and history.

Spitz was quite good in arguing his points, using the subtlety and wit of his Nebraska home. He stood out in a crowd with his tall, lanky figure and salty humor. We met often. At the 1977 Congress in Lund, highlighted by my formal debate with Albert Brandenburg on Luther's success and failure as a reformer, Spitz appeared at the social after the event, carrying a music box with a replica of the Luther statue at Worms (the place of Luther's famous "Here I Stand" speech), playing "A Mighty Fortress is Our God." "See, see," he exclaimed and turned to the Catholic colleagues. "We have finally won the Leipzig Debate!" (Between Luther and John

---

8. See my essay "Wilhelm Dilthey and the Interpretation of History," 58–69. Reprinted in *The Boy*, 148–59.

Eck in 1519, resulting in a verdict favoring Eck). I always appreciated his attempts to find a middle ground—often assisted in a *convivium* (festivity) of good spirits emanating from minds and bottles!

At the 1966 Congress in Finland, I met the most engaging Roman Catholic Luther scholar, **OTTO HERMANN PESCH** (1931–). He was my age and had just completed a gigantic study, *The Theology of Justification of Martin Luther and Thomas Aquina: An Attempt of a Systematic Theological Dialogue* (1967, only in German). This literary dialogue concluded with the judgment that there was an ecumenical rapprochement on justification between these two icons of church history: Thomas presented the doctrine in a cool, objective, "sapiental" manner; Luther did it in a hot, subjective, "existential" way. Scholars who disagreed with Pesch had to work through many volumes of primary and secondary literature in order to refute him. Pesch strengthened his work by a detailed guide to the ecumenical Luther on the occasion of the reformer's five-hundredth birthday in 1983, *A Way to Luther* (*Hinführung zu Luther*, 1982).

Pesch and I have become good friends since our first meeting in Finland. He is the best communicator of Catholic theology I know, and he alerts me to new ways of appreciating Luther as a reformer of the church catholic. Like Pelikan, Pesch views Luther not only as a single-minded advocate of "Scripture," but also as a defender of "tradition," represented by liturgy and spiritual formation. That is why he was called from a Catholic seminary to a new academic chair at the Lutheran faculty of the University of Hamburg to teach Systematic Theology. The Hamburg Luther scholar Bernhard Lohse was his close colleague. In Hamburg, Pesch began to work on a systematic theology of his own, published in three volumes as *Catholic Dogmatic—Based on Ecumenical Experience* (*Katholische Dogmatik aus ökumenischer Erfahrung*, 2008–09).

Pesch was the most refreshing Luther scholar I met. The meeting and lasting friendship fulfilled my longing for a Roman Catholic mind who would bridge the gulf between Protestants and Catholics in my native Austria where my father, a Lutheran pastor, experienced the sad, hostile schism between the two churches. When I dialogue with Pesch, listening to his clear communication of Catholic doctrines, or Protestant theology, I sense a Christian unity that bridges the many unnecessary gaps between our two traditions. Pesch is an extraordinary voice of such a unity in numerous non-scholarly works, ranging from catechisms and other guides for parish life. His sense of humor is revealed in a witty explication of the Brothers Grimm's fairy tale "Red Riding Hood" (*Rotkäppchen*), entitled, *What Big Ears You Have!: The Theologians' Red Riding Hood* (1998). It is the tale about a theological faculty that interprets the fairy tale according to its various disciplines, beginning with systematic theology and ending with an "Epilogue in Heaven: A conversation between Red Riding Hood and the apostles Peter and Paul, with Jesus Christ joining in at the end." Such theological imagination, combined with Pesch's masterful performances on the piano and organ, made him a very valued colleague and friend in my theological education.

10

Lutheran-Catholic Dialogue
(1971–1992)

THE NORTH AMERICAN LUTHERAN Catholic Dialogue was launched in 1965 in the wake of Vatican II; seven selected experts from each side met twice a year; and in its first round it dealt with nine basic church-dividing issues.[1]

The quarterback of the Lutheran team, as it were, was the Yale theologian **GEORGE LINDBECK** (1928–). I knew him at Yale and was eager to work with him because he was an expert of medieval scholastic theology and an official "observer" at Vatican II. He reminded me of an owl with his thick glasses and relaxed stance, smoking a pipe between carefully chosen words, and jogging daily to keep in shape. An expert wordsmith and negotiator, he would find ever new linguistic ways to express thorny issues.

When we began dealing with the complex issue of authority, mired in the dogma of papal infallibility, Lindbeck successfully pushed for a dialogue in two parts: on papal

---

1. 1) The Nicene Creed as dogma, 2) Baptism, 3) The Eucharist as sacrifice, 4) Ministry, 5) Papal primacy, 6) Teaching authority, 7) Justification by faith, 8) The saints and Mary, and 9) Scripture and tradition. See *Lutherans and Catholics in Dialogue* (1965–93).

primacy and on teaching authority. Thus infallibility appeared in a more moderate light. Brainstorming around the problem of infallibility led to the Lutheran proposal of the "indefectibility" of the church, based on Article VII of the Augsburg Confession that "one holy church will remain forever." After the first few rounds of the Dialogue, Lindbeck published an ecumenically optimistic book, *The Future of Roman Catholicism* (1970), followed by a paper for a Catholic audience at Marquette University, published as *Infallibility* (1970). In the Dialogue, he proposed a discussion of "moderate infallibilism" because no dogma can guarantee a teaching without error, due to historical changes; it can, however, protect the church from a definitive separation from Christ. In this context, I coined the phrase "magisterial mutuality," the sharing of ecclesiastical teaching authority. But neither this phrase, nor any other attempt to compromise, was successful, given the eschatological finality of infallible claims.

When we discussed the Lutheran counterpart to papacy, as it were, "justification by faith," and could not find total agreement in the Lutheran team, Lindbeck lost his cool, pounded the desk in our caucus room and exclaimed, "We must find a way." We did, using the Christ-centered language of Luther's explanation of the Second Article of the Apostles' Creed in the Small Catechism; it never mentions "justification," but expresses precisely what it means, namely the unconditional love of God without salvation through merits.[2]

I recall an occasion that defines, albeit in an unusual way, Lindbeck, the man. He called me to ask whether he could borrow a formal suit from me on the occasion of the

2. See *The Book of Concord*, 355:4.

graduation of a niece from Gettysburg. On the way home from a Dialogue, I did a workshop in the parish of one of my former students. I had referred to the visit when I said goodbye to Lindbeck and others at the Dialogue. Lindbeck remembered the name of the pastor and had the good luck of contacting me. Since I always engaged a student for house and dog sitting, Lindbeck was able to get into the house and get dressed for his formal occasion. A few weeks later, he appeared in my driveway and returned the suit on his way to a speaking engagement. His words of thanks were amplified by the smiling remark that he had the good fortune of having my size for clothes!

The Lutheran Church-Missouri Synod theologian **ARTHUR CARL PIEPKORN** (1907–1973) was the dialogue's ecumenist par excellence. He confirmed my growing insight that Lutherans should be called "evangelical Catholics" because they wanted to reform the Catholic Church through the gospel. Consequently, they distinguished between church structures that are divinely instituted (*iure divino,* "by divine right") and those that are part of a human tradition for the sake of witness, a "human right" (*ius* divinum). Piepkorn elaborated this point of view in a seminal essay, "*Ius Divinum* and *Adiaphoron* in Relation to Structural Problems in the Church: The Position of the Lutheran Symbolical Books."[3] He asked both teams to make a careful distinction between any ecclesiastical structure as a "divine right" and one they view as an *adiaphoron* ("a thing that makes no difference"), something that is neither commanded nor prohibited. The conclusion of Piepkorn's

---

3. In *Lutherans and Catholics in Dialogue: Papal Primacy and the Universal Church* (1974), 5:119–27.

paper is like a neurosurgical probe into a brain, trying to diagnose a tumor. I have never encountered a better quest for Christian unity than these words:

> If, and as long as, the difference [between divine and human right] remains irreconcilable, each community must ask itself if its view stands so high in the hierarchy of truths, and is so central in its understanding of the gospel that it must regard this difference as divisive to the point where a common participation in the sacrament of the altar is impossible.

Meeting Piepkorn was like an encounter with a military officer. Piepkorn was indeed a retired army chaplain in the rank of a colonel, having served throughout World War II and some post-war years as Senior Chaplain on the staff of General Omar Bradley and General Dwight D. Eisenhower. He earned thirteen medals, including the Legion of Merit. His civilian uniform was the clerical collar. Moreover, he had a photographic mind, attested by his magnum opus, four volumes of *Profiles of Belief: The Religious Bodies of the United States and Canada* (1977). I recall his impromptu listing of the names of the twelve bishops at the Second Council of Orange in 329; it was mentioned in the Dialogue without, however, using it as a significant source in a discussion about Augustine.

Piepkorn continued to be a dedicated officer in the "church militant." His uniform was a black suit with a clerical collar, bought at a military PX store that sold such suits to officers if they needed civilian clothes. When I once drove him to a PX store to buy a suit, he tried to persuade me to do likewise since the price was well below the cost

Lutheran-Catholic Dialogue

in a commercial store. I was curious how he viewed the move of his church, the Lutheran Church-Missouri Synod, to a biblical Fundamentalism, ending in the adoption of a radical doctrine of inerrancy in 1973. He was opposed to it, and it became quickly known that his stance cost him and others his teaching position at Concordia Seminary and, according to friends, his life through a sudden heart attack. A conservative Catholic member of the Dialogue stated in a newspaper interview that Piepkorn was the most ecumenical theologian in it. I agree with this assessment. He taught me the difference between zealous "ecumeniacs" and realistic ecumenists.

The Lutheran partner **GERHARD FORDE** (1927–2005) represented a point of view that was strictly "evangelical," thus differing from Piepkorn's position. A descendant of Norwegian immigrants, he taught systematic theology at Luther Seminary in St. Paul, Minnesota. Appearing relaxed, with his goatee and slow speech, he looked as if he were ready to soften his views on divisive topics of the Dialogue. But he did not. He stuck to his guns without any explosive polemics and tolerated with humor the label of "a 1521 Fundamentalist" (identifying with Luther's uncompromising "Here I Stand" at the Diet of Worms in 1521). He did, at times, smoke a brand of cigarettes called "Merit." When I asked him whether this was an anti-Catholic gesture, signaling self-righteousness, he responded only with a smile and a big puff on his cigarette!

After a lecture in Gettysburg on Luther's view of freedom, I asked him whether he would be willing to sing with Luther the doctrine of justification, he consented, saying that a celebration or doxology does more justice to it than any other explication.[4] But he became known as an exponent of "radical Lutheranism" because of his definition of Lutheranism as "justification by faith alone." When the Lutheran World Federation and the Roman Catholic Church adopted the "Joint Declaration on the Doctrine of Justification" in 1999,[5] Forde sided with many Lutheran theologians who opposed the Declaration as being theologically inadequate. But the doctrine can never be more than a *declaration* since it is to be proclaimed rather than explained. The "fury of theologians" (*rabies theologorm*), as Luther's friend Melanchthon dubbed the quarrels on the article of justification and its implications for Christian life, has, more often than not, denigrated this precious article of faith. Forde himself offered such a stance in his book *Theology is for Proclamation* (1999). I learned from him and from Gerhard Ebeling, the "father" of the modern Lutheran "theology of the word," not to separate "word" and "sacrament" because the gospel asserts that Christ is "truly present" only in both. But negative learning is a significant tool of theological education. I learned much from the New Testament scholars, the Lutherans **JOHN REUMANN** (1927–2008) and **JOSEPH BURGESS** (1929–); the Catholics **RAYMOND BROWN** (1928–1998) and **JOSEPH FITZMYER** (1920–).

Reumann was a scholar and a churchman, involved in detailed New Testament studies (exemplified in a massive commentary on Philippians) and in almost every affair in his church, The Evangelical Lutheran Church in America (and its predecessors). He was the "teaching theologian"

4. Luther did present the doctrine in his hymn "Dear Christians, one and all, rejoice." See *Lutheran Book of Worship*, no. 299.

5. Text and commentaries in *Joint Declaration on the Doctrine of Justification* (2000).

assigned to many taskforces and assemblies at home and abroad. He collected detailed evidence like a detective in a murder case. Students knew that any record of one of his classes was stored in large metal file cabinets whose contents were later fed into a computer. He also used his love for details in minute word studies in biblical Greek to establish the meaning of the text. When a conversation turned to baseball, Reumann astonished people with numerous memorized scores.

Burgess is the world expert on the meaning of Matt 16:18 ("you are Peter, and on this rock I will build my church"), the decisive Catholic proof-text for the papacy. In a massive doctoral dissertation at the University of Basel, he had worked through the hermeneutical history of this text, showing that it did not support the Catholic claim. Theologically, Burgess tended to agree more with the conservative stance of Forde than with more moderate positions. I appreciated his precision and clarity at times of controversy in the Lutheran caucus. He also did a superb job as one of the editors of the published volumes of the Dialogue.

Brown was on the way to becoming a world-class scholar, focusing on the Gospel of John and on biblical authority in relation to Catholic dogma. He was a member of the Sulpician Order.[6] A large wing of the library of St. Mary's Seminary in Baltimore stores his numerous publications in memory of his graduation. Unfortunately, he left the Dialogue after it had dealt with the papacy in 1971. One could easily guess that he preferred teaching to spending

---

6. Named after the Parish church of St. Sulpice where Jean-Jacques Olier founded a congregation of Roman Catholic priests in 1642, an order without vows, dedicated to seminary education. The "Sulpicians" founded a number of seminaries in Europe and North America.

time in a Dialogue that showed little, if any, progress toward unity. Brown, however, was always cheerful. He relaxed as a lover of operas and moved to Union Seminary in New York to attend them as an aesthetic counter-balance to the ecumenical work at the seminary. He was curious about my love of opera in Vienna during my studies there, and told me how he had enjoyed the musical atmosphere in Vienna.

Fitzmyer worked well with Reumann since he, too, was committed to word study. In addition, he was an expert linguist in Hebrew and Aramaic (the language of Jesus), with the privilege of working on the famous Dead Sea Scrolls. He was the counterpart to Forde, but communicated his views as a Jesuit, erudite and stubborn. But I liked the bit of humor he exhibited when he said, "Pardon me, but my dogmatic slip is showing." He referred to his training at the University of Louvain in Belgium, known for its defensive stance against Luther and Protestantism. When the Dialogue discussed "justification," Fitzmyer criticized the Lutheran view of justification "by faith alone" because the word "alone" was not in the biblical text (Rom 3:28). I used some time to show him Luther's careful reasoning for his translation that tried to preserve the original meaning of faith excluding all "good works." But Fitzmyer remained unconvinced, even though his position echoed a sense of "proof-texting," something he abhorred.

The New Testament experts took on two special assignments that would clarify sensitive, indeed thorny, issues: the significance of Peter and Mary in the New Testament. The four New Testament scholars in the Dialogue invited other Protestant and Catholic experts to join the projects. Brown edited *Peter in the New Testament* (1973); and Fitzmyer edited *Mary in the New Testament* (1978).

I used the results of these studies with success because of their solid research and conclusions based on it. From now on, it could no longer be contended that the New Testament regarded Peter the first "pope," or that Mary was the "co-redeemer" (*co-redemptrix*) in the salvation through Christ. I could not help imagining a third study on *Paul in the New Testament*—all three of the studies could be read with the background music of the contemporary popular trio, "Peter, Paul, and Mary!" A later third study did appear on justification, edited as a massive word study by Reumann and Fitzmyer, *Righteousness in the New Testament: Justification in the Lutheran-Roman Catholic Dialogue in the United States* (1982). I found it less helpful than the other two studies. But "justification," though exalted by Lutherans, never matched the power attributed to Peter and Mary, even though some Lutherans linked the doctrine to a doctrine of biblical inerrancy, thus establishing a "paper pope."

The quarterback of the Catholic team, as it were, was **AVERY DULLES** (1918–2008), the most renowned member of the Dialogue. He was the son of John Foster Dulles, a convert from the Presbyterian Church to Catholicism, a Jesuit theologian and, in his final years, a cardinal. I knew him as a member of Woodstock Faculty in the 1960s, then as a partner on the drafting committee of the Dialogue, and finally as a teaching cardinal at Fordham University. One of my students became his Lutheran assistant while doing doctoral studies at Fordham.

I learned from Dulles how a Jesuit systematic theologian works, especially in an ecumenical Dialogue. Here the witty adage applies as an answer to the question, "How do porcupines make love?" "Very carefully!" Three Dulles books illustrate his careful approach to Christian unity: *Revelation and the Quest for Unity* (1966); *Models of the Church* (1974); and *Models of Revelation* (1983). The drafting committee, consisting of two members from each side (chosen for constructing a "Common Statement" after each round), was often slowed down because Dulles debated a textual formulation, at times even the use of a comma!

Tall, thin, and moving slowly (the effect of polio in his youth), with a Lincoln-like face, Dulles spiked the Dialogue with foreign-language phrases (mostly Latin, German) speaking through his teeth and, at times, with a sudden attack of laughter. I got the impression that he wanted to impress an audience, not because he was a "Dulles"—he disliked flying from Dulles Airport—but because he liked to entertain people. When he was asked what kind of drink he wanted, during a cocktail hour with clergy, he answered, "A diplomat." No one knew this French concoction, and he listed the ingredients for the host. During an official visit as a cardinal in Baltimore he preached a sermon, ending with the assertion that Martin Luther and Ignatius of Loyola (the founder of the Jesuit Order) were the two greatest figures in the sixteenth century. I asked him afterwards, at the luncheon in my home, why he said something I had never heard him say before. He smiled and said, "Well, I saw you sitting there in the first pew and thought that you might be pleased by it."

I respected, indeed admired, Dulles' ecumenical assessment of papal infallibility in a carefully argued paper that tried to redefine Lindbeck's view of "moderate infallibilism." He called papal infallibility "a problematic doctrine that is rather remote from the gospel."[7] That is why it should not be

---

7. Dulles, "Moderate Infallibilism," 6:99.

Lutheran-Catholic Dialogue

used to condemn those who do not accept it. But Dulles did not reject the dogma of infallibility, calling for more discussion leading to reform. He could not go as far as Hans Küng who rejected the dogma.

I never lost contact with Dulles. He remained a friend, also as a cardinal—quite an experience for the son of a Lutheran pastor in Austria who was not allowed to eat his favorite sausage if it was made by the Catholic butcher in the village!

Besides Dulles, there were two other Catholic theologians in the Dialogue, **CARL PETER** (1932–1991) and **GEORGE TAVARD** (1922–2007). They taught me how differentiated Catholic theology can be. Peter was a centrist theologian who clearly articulated the official teachings of his church. Tavard, a native of France, was a committed ecumenist who tried to introduce Catholics to Protestant teachings, especially to Martin Luther; I call him a "closet Lutheran." Peter was a stocky man, vivid in his communication and given to mood swings which, as medical hindsight suggested, signaled progressing cardiac problems causing his untimely death. Tavard, a member of the Order of the Assumption (founded in 1864), was a frail, sensitive man, known as a pastor to many in a variety of denominations; he also was a published author of French poetry.

While working on my Luther book (*Martin—God's Court Jester: Luther in Retrospect*, 1983), the Dialogue had turned to the two most neuralgic issues on both sides: papal infallibility and justification by faith. Peter defended Rome in the context of a "theology of hope," or eschatology which views everything with "eschatological reservation." Thus nothing is perfect until "perfected" after earthly life. Everything is "conditional," and nothing is "unconditional."

Lutherans, however, speak of the Word of God as an "unconditional" promise of salvation based on faith alone. Catholics believe that the truth of the Word of God is "conditioned" by faith in an infallible pope, the representative of Christ on earth.[8] When I asked Peter to endorse my Luther volume he said, "Only if I can eliminate, or at least reduce, your references to 'unconditional' faith in the gospel." I compromised, "Okay. But you must let Luther's references stand." He agreed to endorse the book. But in the dialogue on "justification by faith" Peter insisted that it must be viewed as conditioned by "a critical principle," namely, "Catholic substance" (as Pelikan called it), embodied in formal ecclesiastical teachings.[9] But then, Rome has not yet acknowledged other teachings as authoritative.

A volume of essays and an ecumenical chair honored Peter posthumously at The Catholic University of America in Washington DC. I was the first guest teacher, with a lecture on the Dialogue and a seminar on the theology of Karl Barth. I would have enjoyed more conversations with Peter because he always clearly communicated the distinction between the teachings of his church and his own queries as a theologian and pastor.

Tavard spent his entire career in ecumenical conversations, either "live" as a member of non-Catholic faculties (a long period at a Methodist seminary), or "recorded" in a series of books in various languages. I encountered him first in his book *Holy Writ or Holy Church: The Crisis of the Protestant Reformation* (1959). Then I read *The*

---

8. This complex argumentation is summarized in the memorial essays edited by Phan, *Church and Theology*, 39 and 175–78.

9. See Peter's essay, "Justification by Faith and the Need for Another Principle," 7:304–15.

Pilgrim Church (1967) and, while working in the Dialogue, *Justification: An Ecumenical Study* (1983).

Tavard alerted me to the significance of "tradition" as "memory of the church." I was impressed by the way in which he used this notion of tradition in his historical assessment of specific doctrines. When we discussed the famous bull of Boniface VIII, "Unam Sanctam" (1308), Tavard recommended that we ignore its radical mandate that "it is necessary to salvation for every human creature to be subject to the Roman Pontiff."[10] Since the bull was never truly believed, he contended, it is only an "archeological" object of research. I learned from Tavard that a dogma is without authority if it has not been received, the reception being the work of the Holy Spirit. One could assume that today statistical evidence of a lack of reception by the faithful "proves" the insignificance of a dogma.

When essays were collected to honor Tavard in a commemorative volume, I offered an essay on "Martin Luther's View of Tradition." I was glad to find one occasion when Luther cited the authority of tradition as equal to Scripture. The often-quoted principle "Scripture alone" (*sola scriptura*) was matched by the principle "tradition alone" (*sola traditio*) when Luther defended infant baptism against the claim of radical reformers, the Anabaptists, that only adults should be baptized. One of their principal reasons for taking this position was the lack of evidence for infant baptism in the Bible. Luther, however, insisted on the mandate for infant baptism because the history of the church attested to it. Not Scripture, but the historical memory of the church justifies

---

10. Tavard, "The Bull 'Unam Sanctam' of Boniface VIII," 5:105–19. Quote on p. 107.

infant baptism. What has been practiced so long should not be abolished.[11] That is why Lutherans are not narrow-minded Bible Christians but faithful reformers in the church catholic.

When **JOHANNES CARDINAL WILLEBRANDS** (1909–2006) visited the Dialogue I encountered a "prince of the church" who was a true ecumenist. A Dutchman by birth, Willebrands embodied the spirit of Pope John XXIII who surprised the world by opening the windows of the stuffy Vatican for fresh air and its doors for a radically new dialogue with the world. I was eager to meet the cardinal who rehabilitated Luther as "a teacher we have in common" (*ein gemeinsaner Lehrer*), as he told the assembly of the Lutheran World Federation (LWF) in 1970 in Evian, Switzerland, a year before the four-hundred-fiftieth anniversary of Luther's condemnation by pope and emperor (1521–1971).

He looked like a tall, sturdy middleclass businessman, almost bald, with dark-rimmed glasses, but the traditional dress of his high office. He spoke fluent English, but with the well-known heavy Dutch accent and was well acquainted with our Dialogue. When I asked him about the rumored possibility to lift the ban from Luther, he smiled and repeated what he had told the LWF Assembly, namely, that such a step was "objectively impossible" (*sachlich nicht möglich*); but intensive study of Luther's works, prayer, and other ecumenical activities should be increased between Lutherans and Catholics. A few years after the cardinal's visit to the United States, the Lutheran chair of the Dialogue, George Anderson, and the Presiding Bishop of the Evangelical

11. See Hagen, "Martin Luther's View of Tradition," 61–65. Hagen's offering is included in a collection of essays honoring George H. Tavard. My paper, 65.

Lutheran Church in America, James Crumley, edited a volume of essays honoring Willebrands on his eightieth birthday, *Promoting Unity: Themes in Lutheran-Catholic Dialogue* (1989). My essay was entitled, "Luther: From Rejection to Rehabilitation."

After my retirement from Gettysburg Seminary, I received a phone call from a Catholic publisher of books for lay people. "We do sketches of popular saints," the editor said. "You have been recommended for doing one on Martin Luther." Without revealing my surprise, I responded, "I'd be delighted to do that!" The book was to offer a historical introduction, with selections from Luther's writing. It appeared in 1996 under the title, *Martin Luther: Faith in Christ and the Gospel*. I chose brief selections on "the sense of Scripture," "basic affirmations," "spiritual formation and pastoral care," and "wit and witness."

Other surprises included a call from a nun in Washington, DC, telling me that she and another sister had found a handy paperback edition of three Luther treatises in the library of the Catholic University and that they were intrigued by the treatise on Christian freedom, dedicated to Luther's Pope, Leo X. Would I spend an evening with a group of nuns, with more information about Luther, including news about the pope's reaction? The nuns knew that I was teaching a course on the sixteenth-century Reformation as part of an ecumenical curriculum exchange developed in the 1970s by the "Washington Consortium" of theological schools or seminaries representing Lutherans, Catholics, Anglicans, and Methodists. I volunteered for three evenings. The contact nun told me that I should meet her at one of the entrances to Catholic University; she would wear a red tulip on her habit—an interesting, but unnecessary secular sign of identification (since no other nuns would be waiting at various entrances!). I filed the incident away in my mind as a sign of ecumenical enthusiasm, which diminished when I told the groups that the pope never responded to Luther's tract on Christian freedom.

The Lutheran-Catholic Dialogue was one of my most instructive periods of theological education. To meet with thirteen other participants twice a year for intensive, down-to-earth discussion of topics, often ignored because they were thorny, was an enriching experience. Moreover, I learned to represent my church to Catholics, having to find ways to present my tradition in Catholic terms. The experience illustrated that the quest for Christian unity must involve honest, informed, and enduring dialogue, based on the ecumenical insight that the Holy Spirit grants visible unity only to those who are ready to talk to each other without any reservations.

Although the Lutheran Church-Missouri Synod was represented by two theologians, Piepkorn being one of them, it never agreed with any results of the Dialogue, leaving its best ecumenist in the lurch. In this sense, I had one more lesson in negative learning.

Postscript

I AM GRATEFUL HAVING had sixty memorable theological educators in nearly six decades of academic and spiritual formation. If variety is the spice of life, my career has been like a Hungarian goulash, with its special ingredients, especially red pepper—a savory dish after a long period of simmering.

The red line in my theological education, its rubric, so to speak, highlights a focus on the Christian life as an interim between the ascension of Christ and his return on the last day. I learned that "hope" is the best Christian word and "evil" is the worst. Hope makes everything on earth penultimate, and evil makes all of earthly life "confused" or "diabolical" (from the Greek *diaballein*, "to throw things around"). I learned to think theologically about a future beyond the evils of Adolf Hitler's Nazism, Joseph Stalin's Communism, and the power of greed in American capitalism. It was comforting to know that they were penultimate. The desire to be ultimate is the "original sin" committed by the first settlers in the Garden of Eden; they wanted to be "like God" (Gen 3:5).

A theology of hope, exemplified by Barth and Moltmann, and a "Christian realism" about evil, best represented by Reinhold Niebuhr, were the red lines that alerted me to the dangers of a "realized eschatology," a false hope for building the kingdom of God on earth, confusing "the church militant" with "the church triumphant." Such a theology generates a "toxic spirituality."[1]

Using biblical paradigms for my harvest of theological education, I have become "wise as a serpent and innocent as a dove" (Matt 10:16). This is the mandate of Jesus for his disciples who will have to endure evil which, at its worst, will be sheer terror when family members murder each other and when they will be hated as Christians. But there is the promise that "the one who endures to the end will be saved" (Matt 10:21–22).

The serpent appears first as the instrument of temptation in the story of the Fall, promising Adam and Eve that they would be "like God" (Gen 3:5). Then, the serpent becomes a symbol of salvation from death during the Exodus of the people of Israel. Looking at a bronze serpent saved them from death by poisonous snakes (Num 21:9). Finally, when Nicodemus visited Jesus by night for a discussion of how to be born again, Jesus told him that the bronze serpent is the "Son of Man" who grants salvation to those who believe in him (John 3:14). The serpent is a symbol of healing and salvation, an image associated with the Greek god of healing, Asclepios, whose cult flourished around 420 BCE. He is portrayed with a serpent curled around his staff (the logo of modern medicine), its head touching his left hand. Healing and salvation do not occur without a proper diagnosis leading to a prognosis. "Serpenthood," as it were, is the sharp Christian discernment of evil.

The innocent dove cooing on rooftops represents a child-like faith longing for a never-ending future with God

---

1. The title of my most recent book (2009), describing various Christian traditions representing a destructive "triumphalism."

through Christ. It is sometimes manifested in spiritual gifts, such as "speaking in tongues" (1 Cor 12:10). But cooing doves disregard danger when they make love on rooftops. Consequently, they are shot at close range (as any fowl hunter knows). That is why "dovehood," as it were, must be combined with "serpenthood." The best theologians are those who, like well-trained physicians, can diagnose and treat the spiritual ills in the church, "the body of Christ." At the same time, "doctors of theology" must be grounded in a child-like faith, manifested in prayer and praise.

Karl Barth demonstrated for me the peculiar dialectic of serpent and dovehood. He sharply discerned the lure of evil, be it the political tyranny of Adolf Hitler, Communist ideology, or the greed of capitalism. But he also was a simple child of God, rising every morning with prayer and praise (accompanied by the music of Mozart!).

I decided to become a church historian to tame my drive to be a systematic theologian and arrange my faith in logical loci, in a hierarchy of truth, or in other similar ways. I wanted to concentrate on discerning the "signs of the times" (Matt 16:3) whose interpretations shaped the history of the church. As a Lutheran, exposed to Martin Luther, I learned to respect a strong Christ-centered stance, known as a "theology of the cross." But intensive Luther studies convinced me that his focus on the cross was combined with a focus on the glory of a future without the cross. Thus, his "theology of cross" already has the ring of a "theology of freedom." I see this bi-focal stance as the most important part of my spiritual and academic formation. It created serenity in turbulent times and prepared me for my last day before the last day. So I can sing with the Psalmist, "Those who go out weeping, bearing the seed of sowing, shall come home with shouts of joy, carrying their sheaves" (Ps 126:6).

Bibliography

THE BIBLIOGRAPHY LISTS THE most recent editions of sources cited in the text and in the footnotes.

Ahlstrom, Sidney. *A Religious History of the American People*. New Haven: Yale University Press, 1972.
Bainton, Roland. *Here I Stand: A Life of Martin Luther*. Peabody, ME: Hendrickson, 2009.
———. "The Left Wing of the Reformation." *Journal of Religion* 21 (1941) 124–34.
———. *The Martin Luther Christmas Book: with Celebrated Woodcuts by his Contemporaries*. Philadelphia: Westminster, 1948.
———. *Roly: Chronicles of a Stubborn Non-Conformist* (Autobiography). Edited by Ruth Gritsch. New Haven: Yale Divinity School, 1985. Available only through a contribution to the Roland Bainton Fund.
Barth, Karl. *Church Dogmatics*. Translated and edited by T. F. Torrance and G. W. Bromiley. 14 vols. Edinburgh: T. & T. Clark, 2004.
———. *Epistle to the Romans*. Translation of 2d rev. ed. 1922. New York: Oxford University Press, 1968.
———. *Letters, 1961–1968*. Translated by Geoffrey W. Bromiley. Grand Rapids: Eerdmans, 1981.
———. "Nein! Antwort an Emil Brunner" ("No! Answer to Emil Brunner"). *Theologische Existenz heute* 14 (1934).
———. *Protestant Theology in the Nineteenth Century*. London: SCM Press, 2001.
Bayer, Oswald. *Luther's Theology: A Contemporary Interpretation*. Grand Rapids: Eerdmans, 2008.
———. *Promissio: Geschichte der reformatorischen Wende in Luthers Theologie (Promise: A History of Luther's Theological Break-Through)*. 2d ed. Göttingen: Vadenhoeck & Ruprecht, 1989.
Bernard of Charters in John Salisbury, *The Metalogion*. Edited by C. J. Webb. Translated by Daniel McGary. Berkeley: University of California Press, 1955.

Bloch, Ernst. *Thomas Müntzer als Theologe der Revolution (Thomas Müntzer as a Theologian of Revolution)*. Berlin: Aufbau, 1962.

Bohatec, Joseph. *Calvins Lehre von Staat und Kirche (Calvin's Doctrine of State and Church)*. Breslau: Marcus, 1937.

Bonhoeffer, Dietrich. *The Cost of Discipleship*. Clearwater, FL: Touchstone, 1995.

The Book of Concord: The Confessions of the Evangelical Lutheran Church. Edited by Robert Kolb and Timothy J. Wengert. Minneapolis: Fortress, 2000.

Bornkamm, Heinrich. *Luther and the Old Testament*. Translated by Eric W. and Ruth Gritsch. Philadelphia: Fortress, 1969.

Brecht, Martin. *Martin Luther*. Translated by James L. Schaaf. 3 vols. Minneapolis: Fortress, 1985–99.

Brown, Raymond, et al. *Peter in the New Testament: Collaborative Assessment by Protestant and Roman Catholic Scholars*. Eugene OR: Wipf & Stock, 2002.

Brunner, Emil. *The Divine Imperative*. Cambridge, UK: Lutterworth Press, 2003.

———. *Dogmatics*. 3 vols. Cambridge, UK: James Cark, 2002.

———. *The Great Invitation: Zurich Sermons*. Cambridge, UK: Lutterworth, 2002.

———. *The Misunderstanding of the Church*. Cambridge, UK: Lutterworth, 1954.

———. "Nature and Grace" In *Natural Theology*. Translated by Peter Fraenkel. London: Centenary, 1946. Pp. 17–32.

———. *Truth as Encounter*. Philadelphia: Westminster, 1964.

Bultmann, Rudolf. *Kerygma and Myth*. Edited by H. Bartsch. New York: Harper & Row, 1961.

Cameron, Charles M. "Karl Barth the Preacher." *Evangelical Quarterly* 66:2 (1994) 99–106. Online: http://www.theologicalstudies.org.uk/pdf/eq/barth_cameron.pdf.

Campbell, Will. *Brother to a Dragon Fly*. London: Continuum, 2000.

———. *Cecilia's Sin: A Novella*. Macon, GA: Mercer University Press, 1983.

———. *The Glad River*. Macon, GA: Smyth & Helwys, 2005.

———, and James Holloway. *Up to Our Steeples in Politics*. Eugene, OR: Wipf & Stock, 2004.

Campenhausen, Hans Von. *Ecclesiastical Authority and Spiritual Power in the First Three Centuries*. Peabody, ME: Hendrickson, 1997.

———. *The Formation of the Christian Bible*. Ramsey, NJ: Sigler, 1997.

———. *Theologen Spiess-und Spass, kaum ein halbes Tausend christliche und unchristliche Scherze (Funny Theologians: Almost 500 Christian and non-Christian Jokes)*. Gütersloh: Siebenstern, 1976.

Cullmann, Oskar. *Christ and Time: The Primitive Christian Conception of Time and History*. Philadelphia: Westminster, 1950.

———. *Peter: Disciple, Apostle, Martyr*. Philadelphia: Westminster, 1953.

Dantine, Wilhelm. *Justification of the Ungodly*. Saint Louis: Concordia Publishing House, 1968.

Denbeaux, Fred. *The Art of Christian Doubt*. New York: Association Press, 1960.

Dr. Martin Luthers Werke. Kritische Gesamtausgabe [Schriften]. Weimar: Böhlau, 1883– .

Dulles, Avery. *Models of the Church*. New York: Doubleday, 1991.

———. *Models of Revelation*. New York: Orbis, 1982.

———. "Moderate Infallibilism." In *Lutherans and Catholics in Dialogue*, 6:81–100.

———. *Revelation and the Quest for Unity*. London: Corpus Books, 1968.

Ebeling, Gerhard. *Dogmatik des christlichen Glaubens (Dogmatics of the Christian Faith)*. 3 vols. Tübingen: Mohr-Siebeck, 1993.

———. *Luther: An Introduction to his Thought*. Philadelphia: Fortress, 1970.

———. *Word and Faith*. Philadelphia: Fortress, 1963.

"Editorial: The Strange New World of the Bible." *Theology Today* 43/3 (1986) 412–16.

Eichrodt, Walter. *Die Quellen der Genesis (The Sources of Genesis)*. Giessen: Topelmann, 1916.

———. *Theology of the Old Testament*. 2 vols. Philadelphia: Westminster, 1961.

Fitzmyer, Joseph, ed. *Mary in the New Testament: A Collaborative Assessment by Protestant and Roman Catholic Scholars*. Philadelphia: Fortress, 1978.

Forde, Gerhard. *Theology is for Proclamation*. Minneapolis: Fortress, 1990.

Frankl, Viktor. *Man's Search for Meaning: An Introduction to Logotherapy*. Boston: Beacon, 2006.

———. *The Unconscious God*. New York: Simon & Schuster, 1975.

Gassmann, Günther, ed. *Historical Dictionary of Lutheranism*. Lanham, MD and London: Scarecrow, 2001.

———, and Scott Hendrix. *Fortress Introduction to the Lutheran Confessions*. Minneapolis: Fortress, 1999.

Grane, Leif. *The Augsburg Confession: A Commentary*. Minneapolis: Fortress, 1987.

———. *Modus Loquendi Theologicus: Luthers Kampf um die Erneuerung der Theologie (Luther's Struggle for the Renewal of Theology)*. Leiden: Brill, 1975.

———, and Bernhard Lohse, eds. *Luther und die Theologie der Gegenwart (Luther and Contemporary Theology)*. Göttingen: Vandenhoeck & Ruprecht, 1977.

Gritsch, Eric W. *The Boy from the Burgenland: From Hitler Youth to Seminary Professor*. West Conshohocken, PA: Infinity, 2006.

———, ed. *Encounters with Luther: Lectures, Discussions, and Sermons at the Martin Luther Colloquia*. 4 vols. Gettysburg: Institute for Luther Studies, 1970–90.

———. *A Handbook for Christian Life in the 21st Century*. Delhi, NY: American Lutheran Publicity Bureau, 2005.

———. *A History of Lutheranism*. Minneapolis: Fortress, 2002.

———. "Luther and Violence: A Reappraisal of a Neuralgic Theme." *Sixteenth Century Journal* 3 (1972) 37–55.

———. "Luther: From Rejection to Rehabilitation." In H. George Anderson and James R. Crumley Jr. *Promoting Unity: Themes in Lutheran-Catholic Dialogue*. Minneapolis: Fortress, 1989. Pp. 9–16.

———. "Luther und die Schwärmer: Verworfene Anfechtung? Zum 50. Todesjahr Karl Holl." („Luther and the Radicals: Rejected Challenge? In Commemoration of the 50th Anniversary of the Death of Karl Holl"). *Luther* 3 (1976) 105–21.

———. *Martin—God's Court Jester: Luther in Retrospect*. Eugene, OR: Wipf & Stock, 2009.

———, ed. *Martin Luther: Faith in Christ and the Gospel*. Hyde Park, NY: New City, 1996.

———. "Martin Luther's View of Tradition." In Kenneth Hagen, ed. *Quadrilog. Tradition and the Future of the Church: Essays in Honor of George H. Tavard*. Collegeville, MN: Liturgical, 1994. Pp. 61–75.

———. "Nine and One Half Theses. Presented Out of Love and Zeal for Lutheranism as a Reform Movement Within the Church Catholic, and by Mandate of the Continuation Committee of the Fifth International Congress for Luther Research. Meeting August 14 to 20, 1977 in Lund, Sweden." In *The Boy from the Burgenland*, 317–25.

———. *Reformer Without a Church: The Life and Thought of Thomas Müntzer, 1488?–1525*. Philadelphia: Fortress, 1968.

———. *Thomas Müntzer: A Tragedy of Errors*. Minneapolis: Fortress, 1989. 2d ed. 2007.

———. *Toxic Spirituality: Four Enduring Temptations of Christian Faith*. Minneapolis: Fortress, 2009.

———. "Wilhelm Dilthey and the Interpretation of History." *The Lutheran Quarterly* 15 (1963) 58–69.

———, and Robert W. Jenson. *Lutheranism: The Theological Movement and Its Confessional Writings*. Philadelphia: Fortress, 1976.

Heussi, Karl. *Kompendium der Kirchengeschichte*. 11th rev. ed. Tübingen: Mohr, 1957.

Holborn, Hajo. *A History of Modern Germany*. 3 vols. New York: Knopf, 1964.

Horn, Henry. *Hornucopia: Selected Writings of Henry E. Horn*. Edited by Carl F. W. Ficken. Cambridge: The University Lutheran Association of Greater Boston, 2008.

Jaspers, Karl. *Einführung in die Philosophie (Introduction to Philosophy)*. Munich: Piper, 2004.

———. *The Origin and Goal of History*. Santa Barbara: Greenwood, 1977.

Jenson, Robert W. *Alpha and Omega: A Study in the Theology of Karl Barth*. Eugene, OR: Wipf & Stock, 2002.

———. *Systematic Theology*. 2 vols. New York: Oxford University Press, 2001.

Joint Declaration on the Doctrine of Justification (with other documents). Grand Rapids: Eerdmans, 2000.

Jung, Carl. *Answer to Job*. Princeton: University Press, 1973.

Kübler-Ross, Elizabeth. *On Death and Dying*. Florence, KY: Routledge, 2008.

Küng, Hans. *On Being a Christian*. Montreal: Novalis, 2008.

———. *The Beginning of All Things: Science and Religion*. Grand Rapids: Eerdmans, 2008.

———. *A Global Ethics for Politics and Economics*. New York: Oxford University Press, 1998.

———. *Infallible? An Inquiry*. New York: Doubleday, 1983.

———. *Justification: The Doctrine of Karl Barth and a Catholic Reflection*. Philadelphia: Westminster, 2004.

Lindbeck, George. *The Future of Roman Catholic Theology*. London: SPCK, 1972.

———. *Infallibility*. Milwaukee: Marquette University Press, 1970.

Littell, Franklin, H. *The German Phoenix: Men and Movements in the Church in Germany*. New York: Doubleday, 1960.

Lohse, Bernhard. *Martin Luther's Theology: Its Historical and Systematic Development*. Minneapolis: Fortress, 1999.

Lutheran Book of Worship. Minneapolis: Augsburg Publishing House, 1978.

Lutherans and Catholics in Dialogue. Edited by Paul Empie, T. A. Murphy et al. 9 vols. Minneapolis: Augsburg Publishing House, 1965–1993.

Luther's Works. American Edition. 55 vols. Philadelphia Fortress and St. Louis: Concordia, 1955–1986.

Mannermaa, Tuomo. *Christ Present in Faith: Luther's View of Justification*. Minneapolis: Fortress, 2005.

Mathonnet-VanderWell, Steven. "Interview with I. John Hesselink." *Perspectives* (October 2007). No Pages. Online: http://www.rca.org/Page.aspx?pid=3445.

Moltmann, Jürgen. *The Church and the Power of the Spirit: A Contribution to Messianic Ecclesiology*. London: SCM, 1975.

———. *The Crucified God: The Cross of Christ as the Foundation and Criticism of Christian Theology*. London: SCM, 1973.

———. *Theology of Hope: On the Ground and the Implications of a Christian Eschatology*. London: SCM, 1967.

Niebuhr, Reinhold. *The Irony of American History*. Chicago: University Press, 2008.

———. *Leaves From the Notebook of a Tamed Cynic*. Philadelphia: Westminster, 1990.

———. *The Nature and Destiny of Man*. 2 vols. New York: Charles Scribner's Sons, 1964.

Niebuhr, Richard. *Christ and Culture*. New York: Harper, 1951.

———. *The Kingdom of God in America*. New York: Harper Torchbooks, 1959.

———. *The Social Sources of Denominationalism*. Cleveland: World Publishing Company, 1965.

Oberman, Heiko, A. *The Harvest of Medieval Theology*. Grand Rapids: Baker Academic, 2001.

———. *Luther: Man Between God and the Devil*. New Haven: Yale University Press, 1990.

———. *The Roots of Anti-Semitism: In the Age of Renaissance and Reformation*. Minneapolis: Fortress, 1984.

Oxford Encyclopedia of the Reformation. Edited by Hans J. Hillerbrand. 4 vols. Oxford: University Press, 1996.

Pannenberg, Wolfhart. *Jesus: God and Man*. Philadelphia: Westminster, 1968.

———. *Revelation as History*. New York: Macmillan, 1969.

———. *Systematic Theology*. 3 vols. Edinburgh: T. & T. Clark, 1998.

"Paul Tillich, Lover." *Time* (October 8, 1973). No Pages. Online: http://www.time.com/time/magazine/article/0,9171,908007,00.html.

Pelikan, Jaroslav. *The Christian Tradition*. 5 vols. Chicago: University Press, 1997.

———. *Obedient Rebels: Catholic Substance and Protestant Principle in Luther's Reformation*. London: SDCM, 1964.

Pesch, Otto Hermann. *Hinführung zu Luther (A Way to Luther)*. 3d rev. ed. Mainz: Matthias Grünewald, 2004.

———. *Katholische Dogmatik: Aus ökumenischer Erfahrung (Catholic Dogmatics: Based on Ecumenical Experience)*. 2 vols. Mainz: Matthias Grünewald Verlag, 2008–2009.

———. *Theologie der Rechtfertigung bei Martin Luther und Thomas von Aquin: Versuch eines systematisch-theologischen Dialogs (The Theology of justification of Martin Luther and Thomas Aquinas: An Attempt of a Systematic-Theological Dialogue)*. 2d ed. Mainz: Matthias Grünewald, 1985.

———. *What Big Ears You Have! The Theologians' Red Riding Hood*. Collegeville, MN: Liturgical, 2000.

Peter, Carl. "Justification by Faith and the Need for Another Principle." In *Lutherans and Catholics in Dialogue*, 7:304–15.

Phan, Peter C., ed. *Church and Theology: Essays in Memory of Carl J. Peter*. Washington DC: Catholic University Press, 1995.

Piepkorn, Arthur, C. "*Ius Divinum* and *Adiaphoron* in Relation to Structural Problems in the Church: The Position of the Lutheran Symbolical Books." In *Lutherans and Catholics in Dialogue*, 5:119–27.

———. *Profiles in Belief. The Religious Bodies of the United States and Canada*. New York: Harper & Row, 1977.

Pinomaa, Lennart. *Anfechtung als Hintergrund des Evangeliums in der Theologie Luthers (Temptation as the Background of the Gospel in Luther's Theology)*. Helsinki: Finnische Akademie der Wissenschaften, 1943.

———. *Faith Victorious: An Introduction to Luther's Theology*. Philadelphia: Fortress, 1963.

Prenter, Regin. *Spiritus Creatus*. Eugene, OR: Wipf & Stock, 2001.

Reumann, John, ed. *Righteousness in the New Testament: Justification in the United States Lutheran-Roman Catholic Dialogue*. Minneapolis: Fortress, 1982.

Schaff, Philip, ed. *Creeds of Christendom*. 3 vols., 6th ed. Grand Rapids: Eerdmans, 1990.

Schweizer, Eduard. *Church Order in the New Testament*. Eugene, OR: Wipf & Stock, 2006.

Spitz, Lewis. *Luther and German Humanism*. Farnham, UK: Variorum, 1996.

———. *The Renaissance and Reformation Movements*. Bronxville, NY: Concordia College, 2003.

Stendahl, Krister. "The Apostle Paul and the Introspective Conscience of the West." *The Harvard Theological Review* 56 (1963) 199–215.

———. *Paul Among Jews and Gentiles*. Philadelphia: Fortress, 1976.

———. *The School of St. Matthew*. Ramsey, NJ: Sigler, 1991.

Tavard, George. "The Bull 'Unam Sanctam' of Boniface VIII." In *Lutherans and Catholics in Dialogue*, 5:105–19.

———. *Holy Writ or Holy Church: The Crisis of the Protestant Reformation*. New York: Harper Brothers, 1959.

———. *Justification: An Ecumenical Study*. Mahwah, NJ: Paulist, 1983.

———. *Pilgrim Church*. Saint Louis: Herder & Herder, 1967.

Tillich, Paul. *The Courage to Be*. New Haven: Yale University Press, 2000.

———. *Systematic Theology*. 3 vols. Chicago: University Press, 1967.

Troeltsch, Ernst. *The Social Teaching of the Christian Churches*. 2 vols. Philadelphia: Westminster John Knox, 1992.

Vogel, Heinrich. *Die Krisis des Schönen (The Crisis of the Beautiful)*. Berlin, 1931.

———. *Gott in Christo (God in Christ)*. Berlin, 1951.

Welch, Claude. *In This Name: The Doctrine of the Trinity in Contemporary Theology*. New York: Charles Scribner's Sons, 1952.

———. *Protestant Thought in the Nineteenth Century*. Vol 1: 1799–1870. New Haven: Yale University Press, 1972. Vol. 2: 1870–1914. New Haven: University Press, 1985.

Wentz, Abdel Ross. *A Basic History of Lutheranism in America*. 2d rev. ed. Philadelphia: Fortress, 1964.

Wentz, Frederick K. *Expanding Horizons for America's Lutherans: The Story of Abdel Ross Wentz*. Gettysburg: Seminary Ridge, 2009.

Willebrands, Johannes Cardinal. "Gesandt in die Welt" ("Sent into the World") *Lutherische Rundschau* 20 (1970) 447–60.

Williams, George H. *The Mind of John Paul II: Origins of His Thought and Action*. New York: Seabury, 1981.

———. *The Radical Reformation*. 3d rev. ed. Kirksville, MO: Truman State University: University Press, 2001.

———. *Wilderness and Paradise in Christian Thought*. New York: Harper & Brothers, 1962.

———, and Angel M. Mergal, eds. *Anabaptist and Spiritual Writers*. The Library of Christian Classics 25. Philadelphia: Westminster, 1957.

Wingren, Gustaf. *Creation and Law*. Eugene, OR: Wipf & Stock, 2003.

———. *Luther on Vocation*. Eugene, OR: Wipf & Stock, 2004.

With One Voice: A Lutheran Resource for Worship. Minneapolis: Augsburg, 1995.

www.ingramcontent.com/pod-product-compliance
Lightning Source LLC
Chambersburg PA
CBHW060824190426
43197CB00038B/2208